Reanimating Democracy
A HISTORY & GUIDE
for ORGANIZING a
NONVIOLENT PROTEST

by

Trace Burroughs

Published by ThePeopleGov.org
(Send a message each day to 100 different State and
or Federal representatives in 2 seconds.)
©Burroughs Media 2014

Quotes About Nonviolence

"Anger is the enemy of non-violence and pride is a monster that swallows it up."
-*Mahatma Gandhi*

"Non-violence leads to the highest ethics, which is the goal of all evolution.
Until we stop harming all other living beings, we are still savages."
-*Thomas A. Edison*

"At the center of non-violence stands the principle of love."
-*Martin Luther King, Jr.*

"There is no such thing as defeat in non-violence."
-*Cesar Chavez*

"Non-violence is not glamorous, and you don't see the effects right away.."
-*Julia Bacha*

Table of Contents

History of Nonviolence

The use of nonviolence runs throughout history. There have been numerous instances of people courageously and nonviolently refusing cooperation with injustice. However, the fusion of organized mass struggle and nonviolence is relatively new. It originated largely with Mohandas Gandhi in 1906 at the onset of the South African campaign for Indian rights. Later, the Indian struggle for complete independence from the British Empire included a number of spectacular nonviolent campaigns. Perhaps the most notable was the year-long Salt campaign in which 100,000 Indians were jailed for deliberately violating the Salt Laws.

The refusal to counter the violence of the repressive social system with more violence is a tactic that has also been used by other movements. The militant campaign for women's suffrage in Britain included a variety of nonviolent tactics such as boycotts, noncooperation, limited property destruction, civil disobedience, mass marches and demonstrations, filling the jails, and disruption of public ceremonies.

The Salvadoran people have used nonviolence as one powerful and necessary element of their struggle. Particularly during the 1960s and 70s, Christian based communities, labor unions, campesino organizations, and student groups held occupations and sit-ins at universities, government offices, and places of work such as factories and haciendas.

There is rich tradition of nonviolent protest in this country as well, including Harriet Tubman's underground railroad during the civil war and Henry David Thoreau's refusal to pay war taxes. Nonviolent civil disobedience was a critical factor in gaining women the right to vote in the United States, as well.

The U.S. labor movement has also used nonviolence with striking effectiveness in a number of instances, such as the Industrial Workers of the World (IWW) free speech confrontations, the Congress of Industrial Organizations (CIO) sitdown strikes from

1935-1937 in auto plants, and the UFW grape and lettuce boycotts.

Using mass nonviolent action, the civil rights movement changed the face of the South. The Congress of Racial Equality (CORE) initiated modern nonviolent action for civil rights with sit-ins and a freedom ride in the 1940s. The successful Montgomery bus boycott electrified the nation. Then, the early 1960s exploded with nonviolent actions: sit-ins at lunch counters and other facilities, organized by the Student Nonviolent Coordinating Committee (SNCC); Freedom Rides to the South organized by CORE; the nonviolent battles against segregation in Birmingham, Alabama, by the Southern Christian Leadership Conference (SCLC); and the 1963 March on Washington, which drew 250,000 participants.

Opponents of the Vietnam War employed the use of draft card burnings, draft file destruction, mass de-. monstrations (such as the 500,000 who turned out in 1969 in Washington, D.C.), sit-ins, blocking induction centers, draft and tax resistance, and the historic 1971 May Day traffic blocking in Washington, D.C. in which 13,000 people were arrested.

Since the mid-70s, we have seen increasing nonviolent activity against the nuclear arms race and nuclear power industry. Nonviolent civil disobedience actions have taken place at dozens of nuclear weapons research installations, storage areas, missile silos, test sites, military bases, corporate and government offices and nuclear power plants. In the late 1970s mass civil disobedience actions took place at nuclear power plants from Seabrook, New Hampshire to the Diablo Canyon reactor in California and most states in between in this country and in other countries around the world. In 1982, 1750 people were arrested at the U.N. missions of the five major nuclear powers. Mass actions took place at the Livermore Laboratories in California and SAC bases in the midwest. In the late 80s a series of actions took place at the Nevada test site. International disarmament actions changed world opinion about nuclear weapons.

In 1980 women who were concerned with the destruction of the

Earth and who were interested in exploring the connections between feminism and nonviolence were coming together. In November of 1980 and 1981 the Women's Pentagon Actions, where hundreds of women came together to challenge patriarchy and militarism, took place. A movement grew that found ways to use direct action to put pressure on the military establishment and to show positive examples of life-affirming ways to live together. This movement spawned women's peace camps at military bases around the world from Greenham Common, England to Puget Sound Peace Camp in Washington state, with camps in Japan and Italy among others.

The anti-apartheid movement in the 80s has built upon the powerful and empowering use of civil disobedience by the civil rights movement in the 60s. In November of 1984, a campaign began that involved daily civil disobedience in front of the South African Embassy. People, including members of Congress, national labor and religious leaders, celebrities, students, community leaders, teachers, and others, risked arrest every weekday for over a year. In the end over 3,100 people were arrested protesting apartheid and U.S. corporate and government support. At the same time, support actions for this campaign were held in 26 major Cities, resulting in an additional 5,000 arrests.

We also saw civil disobedience being incorporated as a key tactic in the movement against intervention in Central America. Beginning in 1983, national actions at the White House and State Department as well as local actions began to spread. In November 1984, the Pledge of Resistance was formed. Since then, over 5,000 people have been arrested at military installations, congressional offices, federal buildings, and CIA offices. Many people have also broken the law by providing sanctuary for Central American refugees and through the Lenten Witness, major denomination representatives have participated in weekly nonviolent civil disobedience actions at the Capitol.

Student activists have incorporated civil disobedience in both their anti-apartheid and Central America work. Divestment became the

campus slogan of the 80s. Students built shantytowns and staged sit-ins at Administrator's offices. Hundreds have been arrested resulting in the divestment of over 130 campuses and the subsequent withdrawal of over $4 billion from the South African economy. Central America student activists have carried out campaigns to protest CIA recruitment on campuses. Again, hundreds of students across the country have been arrested in this effort.

Nonviolent direct action has been an integral part of the renewed activism in the lesbian and gay community since 1987, when ACT UP (AIDS Coalition to Unleash Power) was formed. ACT UP and other groups have organized hundreds of civil disobedience actions across the country, focusing not only on AIDS but on the increasing climate of homophobia and attacks on lesbians and gay men. On October 13, 1987, the Supreme Court was the site of the first national lesbian and gay civil disobedience action, where nearly 600 people were arrested protesting the decision in Hardwick vs. Bowers, which upheld sodomy laws. This was the largest mass arrest in D.C. since 1971.

Analysis

Power itself is not derived through violence, though in governmental form it is usually violent in nature. Governmental power is often maintained through oppression and the tacit compliance of the majority of the governed. Any significant withdrawal of that compliance will restrict or dissolve governmental control. Apathy in the face of injustice is a form of violence. Struggle and conflict are often necessary to correct injustice.

Our struggle is not easy, and we must not think of nonviolence as a "safe" way to fight oppression. The strength of nonviolence comes from our willingness to take personal risk without threatening other people.

The Basic Elements of Nonviolence

Dr. Martin Luther King, Jr. wrote that the philosophy and practice of nonviolence has six basic elements.

1. nonviolence is resistance to evil and oppression. It is a human way to fight.

2. It does not seek to defeat or humiliate the opponent, but to win his/ her friendship and understanding.

3. The nonviolent method is an attack on the forces of evil rather than against persons doing the evil. It seeks to defeat the evil and not the persons doing the evil and injustice.

4. It is the willingness to accept suffering without retaliation.

5. A nonviolent resister avoids both external physical and internal spiritual violence- not only refuses to shoot, but also to hate, an opponent. The ethic of real love is at the center of nonviolence.

6. The believer in nonviolence has a deep faith in the future and the forces in the universe are seen to be on the side of justice.

198 Methods of Nonviolent Action

Practitioners of nonviolent struggle have an entire arsenal of "non-violent weapons" at their disposal. Listed below are 198 of them, classified into three broad categories: nonviolent protest and persuasion, noncooperation (social, economic, and political), and nonviolent intervention. A description and historical examples of each can be found in volume two of The Politics of Nonviolent Action by Gene Sharp.

The Methods of Nonviolent Protest and Persuasion

Formal Statements
1. Public Speeches
2. Letters of opposition or support
3. Declarations by organizations and institutions
4. Signed public statements
5. Declarations of indictment and intention
6. Group or mass petitions

Communications with a Wider Audience
7. Slogans, caricatures, and symbols
8. Banners, posters, and displayed communications
9. Leaflets, pamphlets, and books
10. Newspapers and journals
11. Records, radio, and television
12. Skywriting and earthwriting

Group Representations
13. Deputations
14. Mock awards
15. Group lobbying
16. Picketing
17. Mock elections

Symbolic Public Acts
18. Displays of flags and symbolic colors

19. Wearing of symbols
20. Prayer and worship
21. Delivering symbolic objects
22. Protest disrobings
23. Destruction of own property
24. Symbolic lights
25. Displays of portraits
26. Paint as protest
27. New signs and names
28. Symbolic sounds
29. Symbolic reclamations
30. Rude gestures

Pressures on Individuals
31. "Haunting" officials
32. Taunting officials
33. Fraternization
34. Vigils

Drama and Music
35. Humorous skits and pranks
36. Performances of plays and music
37. Singing

Processions
38. Marches
39. Parades
40. Religious processions
41. Pilgrimages
42. Motorcades

Honoring the Dead
43. Political mourning
44. Mock funerals
45. Demonstrative funerals
46. Homage at burial places

Public Assemblies
47. Assemblies of protest or support
48. Protest meetings
49. Camouflaged meetings of protest
50. Teach-ins

Withdrawal and Renunciation
51. Walk-outs
52. Silence
53. Renouncing honors
54. Turning one's back
The Methods of Social Noncooperation

Ostracism of Persons
55. Social boycott
56. Selective social boycott
57. Lysistratic nonaction
58. Excommunication
59. Interdict

Noncooperation with Social Events, Customs, and Institutions
60. Suspension of social and sports activities
61. Boycott of social affairs
62. Student strike
63. Social disobedience
64. Withdrawal from social institutions

Withdrawal from the Social System
65. Stay-at-home
66. Total personal noncooperation
67. "Flight" of workers
68. Sanctuary
69. Collective disappearance
70. Protest emigration (hijrat)
The Methods of Economic Noncooperation: Economic Boycotts

Actions by Consumers
71. Consumers' boycott

Symbolic Strikes
97. Protest strike
98. Quickie walkout (lightning strike)

Agricultural Strikes
99. Peasant strike
100. Farm Workers' strike

Strikes by Special Groups
101. Refusal of impressed labor
102. Prisoners' strike
103. Craft strike
104. Professional strike

Ordinary Industrial Strikes
105. Establishment strike
106. Industry strike
107. Sympathetic strike

Restricted Strikes
108. Detailed strike
109. Bumper strike
110. Slowdown strike
111. Working-to-rule strike
112. Reporting "sick" (sick-in)
113. Strike by resignation
114. Limited strike
115. Selective strike

Multi-Industry Strikes
116. Generalized strike
117. General strike

Combination of Strikes and Economic Closures
118. Hartal
119. Economic shutdown
The Methods of Political Noncooperation

Rejection of Authority
120. Withholding or withdrawal of allegiance
121. Refusal of public support
122. Literature and speeches advocating resistance

Citizens' Noncooperation with Government
123. Boycott of legislative bodies
124. Boycott of elections
125. Boycott of government employment and positions
126. Boycott of government departments, agencies, and other bodies
127. Withdrawal from government educational institutions
128. Boycott of government-supported organizations
129. Refusal of assistance to enforcement agents
130. Removal of own signs and placemarks
131. Refusal to accept appointed officials
132. Refusal to dissolve existing institutions

Citizens' Alternatives to Obedience
133. Reluctant and slow compliance
134. Nonobedience in absence of direct supervision
135. Popular nonobedience
136. Disguised disobedience
137. Refusal of an assemblage or meeting to disperse
138. Sitdown
139. Noncooperation with conscription and deportation
140. Hiding, escape, and false identities
141. Civil disobedience of "illegitimate" laws

Action by Government Personnel
142. Selective refusal of assistance by government aides
143. Blocking of lines of command and information
144. Stalling and obstruction
145. General administrative noncooperation
146. Judicial noncooperation
147. Deliberate inefficiency and selective noncooperation by enforcement agents
148. Mutiny

Domestic Governmental Action
149. Quasi-legal evasions and delays
150. Noncooperation by constituent governmental units

International Governmental Action
151. Changes in diplomatic and other representations
152. Delay and cancellation of diplomatic events
153. Withholding of diplomatic recognition
154. Severance of diplomatic relations
155. Withdrawal from international organizations
156. Refusal of membership in international bodies
157. Expulsion from international organizations
The Methods of Nonviolent Intervention

Psychological Intervention
158. Self-exposure to the elements
159. The fast
a) Fast of moral pressure
b) Hunger strike
c) Satyagrahic fast
160. Reverse trial
161. Nonviolent harassment

Physical Intervention
162. Sit-in
163. Stand-in
164. Ride-in
165. Wade-in
166. Mill-in
167. Pray-in
168. Nonviolent raids
169. Nonviolent air raids
170. Nonviolent invasion
171. Nonviolent interjection
172. Nonviolent obstruction
173. Nonviolent occupation

Social Intervention
174. Establishing new social patterns
175. Overloading of facilities
176. Stall-in
177. Speak-in
178. Guerrilla theater
179. Alternative social institutions
180. Alternative communication system

Economic Intervention
181. Reverse strike
182. Stay-in strike
183. Nonviolent land seizure
184. Defiance of blockades
185. Politically motivated counterfeiting
186. Preclusive purchasing
187. Seizure of assets
188. Dumping
189. Selective patronage
190. Alternative markets
191. Alternative transportation systems
192. Alternative economic institutions

Political Intervention
193. Overloading of administrative systems
194. Disclosing identities of secret agents
195. Seeking imprisonment
196. Civil disobedience of "neutral" laws
197. Work-on without collaboration
198. Dual sovereignty and parallel government

Source: Sharp, Gene. The Politics of Nonviolent Action (3 Vols.), Boston: Porter Sargent, 1973. Provided courtesy of the Albert Einstein Institution.

Are Nonviolent Protests Effective? 13 Case Studies

1. Cherokee Indian Resistance to Forced Relocation (1838)

Objective: Avoid having their land seized by the United States government

Method of Protest: Cherokees stood their ground, and made no preparations to move.

Results: U.S. troops destroyed the homes and property of the resisting Cherokees, forcing them to move west on a journey that would leave approximately 4,000 dead from disease and starvation.

Was the Protest a Success? No. The path the Cherokees took from their homes is still knows as the Trail of Tears.

2. Gandhi's Salt March (1930)

Objective: Independence of Colonial India from British Authority

Method of Protest: To avoid paying the British tax on salt, Gandhi decided to get his own salt. To do this, he walked 240 miles over the course of 24 days, joined by a growing number of followers.

Results: Gandhi was jailed, but the protest drew national attention to his cause and he was eventually released.

Was the Protest a Success? Not immediately, but it is considered a watershed moment for India's struggle for independence, which was finally obtained two decades later.

3. The White Rose Resistance (1942–1943)

Objective: Undermine the Nazi Rule of Germany

Method of Protest: Distributing leaflets that philosophically challenged the ideas of the Nazis.

Results: The six main members of the group were arrested and beheaded.

Was the Protest a Success? No

4. The Montgomery Bus Boycott (1955–1956)

Objective: Lessen racial segregation and inequality for blacks in the American South

Method of Protest: Montgomery's black population refused to use public transportation.

Results: An Alabama district court ruled that the racial segregation was unlawful. The decision was appealed but upheld by the Supreme Court.

Was the Protest a Success? Yes. It also served as the impetus for the civil rights movement of the 1960s.

5. The Kent State Demonstrations (1970)

Caitlin Mirra / Shutterstock.com

Objective: Get President Nixon to stop the invasion of Cambodia and end the war in Vietnam

Method of Protest: Four days of protests and marches

Results: The National Guard fired 67 rounds into the demonstration, killing four and injuring nine.

Was the Protest a Success? Hard to say. While there were no immediate changes in U.S. foreign policy, it did spark many additional protests across the country, which may have had a hand in ending the war.

6. The Tree Sitters of Pureora (1978)

Objective: Stop deforestation of the Pureora forest in New Zealand

Method of Protest: Built tree houses, refused to leave them

Results: The Government agreed to permanently stop logging operations and the area became a park.

Was the Protest a Success? Yes. It has also inspired many other tree-sitting protests, with varying levels of success.

7. Tiananmen Square Protests (1989)

Objective: Political reform and free media in the authoritarian Chinese government

Method of Protest: Seven weeks of peaceful marches and demonstrations

Results: The People's Liberation Army of China opened fire on the protesters. The exact death toll of the massacre is still unknown; estimates range from 200 and 10,000.

Was the Protest a Success? No. The current Chinese government does not acknowledge the killings. All online information about the massacre is censored in China.

8. The Lust Lady Strike of San Francisco (1997)

Objective: Ability for strippers at San Francisco's Lusty Lady club to form a union

Method of Protest: Strippers went on strike protesting outside the club and asking patrons not to enter unless the women were allowed to form a union.

Results: After a lengthy legal battle, the dancers were permitted to form a union

Was the Protest a Success? Yes

9. The Singing Revolution (1986-1991)

Objective: Independence from the former Soviet Union for Estonia, Latvia and Lithuania

Method of Protest: Protesters gathered in the streets where they sang songs of national pride, which had been outlawed by the Soviet occupiers.

Results: After four years of demonstrations, many involving song, and the deaths of 14 protesters in Lithuania, all three countries gained sovereignty.

Was the Protest a Success? Yes

10. Demonstration against Invading Iraq (2003)

Objective: Stop the United States from invading Iraq

Method of Protest: An estimated 6 to 10 million people around the world publicly protested the impending war.

Results: The invasion of Iraq happened anyway.

Was the Protest a Success? No. We still have troops in Iraq to this day.

11. The "Lactivists" at Applebee's (2007)

Objective: Stop discrimination against public breastfeeding at Applebee's Restaurants

Method of Protest: A "Nurse-in" was scheduled — across the country, breastfeeding mothers would nurse their infants in plain view of Applebee's.

Results: Applebee's put out a statement saying "This situation has provided an opportunity for us to work with our associates to ensure we're making nursing mothers feel welcome....we will also accommodate other guests who would be more comfortable moving to another area of the restaurant."

Was the Protest a Success? Yes

12. The Wisconsin Teachers Strike (2011)

Objective: Keep collective bargaining rights for teachers unions in Wisconsin

Method of Protest: For nearly five months, public demonstrations of as many as 100,000 protesters gathered at the Wisconsin Capitol Building.

Results: The Wisconsin Budget Repair Bill, which stripped collective bargaining rights from teachers, was not repealed.

Was the Protest a Success? No, though there are still several lawsuits pending against the bill.

13. The Nuts of Jericho (2007)

Objective: Get the post-apocalyptic TV show Jericho renewed for a second season

Method of Protest: In reference to a scene in the season finale, Jericho fans sent over 20 tons of assorted nuts to the offices of the CBS executives who had canceled the show.

Results: The show was renewed for a second season.

Was the Protest a Success? Yes, though Jericho was again canceled after the second season. The third season was released as a series of comic books.

Planning a Nonviolent Demonstration

Most groups do at least some planning prior to their demonstration. In addition to deciding the choreography of the demonstration, your group should plan whether to obtain a police permit, whether and how to include a "civil disobedience", and other practical matters. If you are unsure about your rights it's a good idea to discuss your plans with an attorney. (An attorney from the Mass Defense Committee is usually available to do this.)

Topics Below

* Deciding whether to obtain a permit

* Bring identification, not contraband

* Civil disobedience and who whould avoid it

* Usual civil disobedience charges and release from precinct

* Be aware of "going through the system"

* Designate a civil disobedience monitor

Deciding whether to obtain a permit.

Permits should be obtained if the demonstration is going to involve a bullhorn or any other electronically amplified sound. A permit should be considered for any demonstration that will be large (more than 100 persons or so) or will move from one place to another. If a permit is not obtained, the police, who will inevitably appear, may drastically curtail the action or prohibit it altogether.

Obviously the issuance of a permit alerts the police to the demonstration and guarantees their presence and usually their advance placement of wooden barricades at the demonstration site (where

the police want them). However, even if a permit is not obtained, the police will appear anyway and although they may allow the demonstration to continue, they may be more intolerant than they would otherwise have been.

If a permit is denied, we recommend that the group call an attorney. She or he may be able to obtain the permit either by re-requesting it at the precinct or by going to court.

Bring identification, not contraband

Persons planning on being arrested should have police-acceptible identification. After the arrest the police transport the arrestee to a police precinct for processing. Unless the charge is a felony, the demonstrator will probably be released as long as her or his identification gives the police reasonable assurance that they know who the person is and where she or he lives. The best identification is a picture driver's license, but most official-looking identifications issued by an agency, organization or company will usually do. The purpose of learning the address is that, in the event that the demonstrator does not appear in court on the scheduled court date, the authorities could find him or her if they tried (which they would probably never do for a demonstration arrest).

Persons planning on being arrested will be at least superficially searched. If the police discover illegal drugs or anything else illegal they will probably not release the person and will add on additional charges.

Civil disobedience and who should avoid it

Originally civil disobedience meant disobeying laws one felt were fundamentally wrong; it has come to mean disobeying any law in protest of something. In planning a civil disobedience it is most important that those planning to be arrested be made aware of the legal and practical consequences of arrest (see below). They should learn the probable arrest charges the police will give and the probable outcomes they will receive in court. Potential

arrestees should also be taught how to minimize the risks of extended police custody by avoiding certain charges, carrying reliable identification and having support at the police precinct.

Persons with outstanding warrants are advised not to get arrested because the warrant may cause the police not to release them from the police precinct. Also, arrest presents risks to non-citizens. While the police do not yet specifically screen arrested persons for immigration issues or automatically communicate with the Immigration and Naturalization Service, non-citizens are required to explain arrests (not just convictions) on many INS applications. Similarly, persons who later may want to apply for jobs involving the government, security or child care may be investigated or asked about arrests, not just convictions, and therefore should weigh participation in a CD very carefully.

Usual civil disobedience charges and release from the precinct.

The most common charges against demonstrators are Disorderly Conduct and Trespass. Basically Disoderly Conduct means about what it sounds like it means -- acting in a manner the police find disorderly -- and Trespass means being present on property without the permission of the rightful custodian of the property. These charges are both "violations" meaning they are not crimes and are about as serious as a moving traffic violation. For these offenses the arrestee is almost always released from the police precinct after being given a ticket informing him or her where and when to go to court.

The next most common charge is Resisting Arrest, which means that the arrestee allegedly exerted force to prevent the police from effecting arrest. (A demonstrator might be given this charge if a police officer uses unreasonable force since the officer wants to establish an excuse for using force.) This offense is a crime, an "A" misdemeanor (and therefore affords the demonstrator to the right to a jury trial). A person is usually released from the precinct with this charge but has a greater chance of being held until court than the above charges.

The courts do not agree on whether or not "going limp" and forcing police to pick up a demonstrator constitutes resisting arrest. Therefore, while persons who go limp risk a Resisting Arrest conviction, there is also legal authority that that is not sufficient conduct to prove Resisting Arrest.

The next most common charge is Riot in the second degree which relates to urging 4 or more persons to to cause property damage or personal injury, or participating in the damage or injury. If there are more than 10 persons involved and there is an injury (including injury to the a police person) or damage, the charge will be a felony - Riot in the first degree - and the arrestee will not be released from the precinct.

Be aware of "going through the system"

Those arrested persons not released at the precinct go "through the system", meaning that they remain in police custody up to the time 24 to 72 hours later when they see a judge in court. The journey involves at least one police precinct, a place called Central Booking (a pre-court clearing house for all the county's arrestees), a mass pen in the court building, and finally a court "pen" where the arrestee will be allowed to speak to an attorney. (All persons are assigned an attorney unless they already have one.) The judge decides whether to release or detain the arrestee until the next court date; most demonstrator defendants are released. The through-the-system experience is one to be avoided. (For example, see Tom Wolfe's only slightly exaggerated description in the novel Bonfire of the Vanities.)

Designate a civil disobedience monitor

Whenever arrests are expected, the demonstration group should appoint a person to monitor the arrests. This person should make sure the arrestees have good identification, keep of list of the persons arrested and, if possible, go to the police precinct to make sure things go well there. The monitor should bring paper and pencil to the demonstration and be prepared to make notes. If there is

police brutality, the monitor should record the incidents, the names of witnesses and the names of the officers involved. A camera is also helpful for such events.

What to do if you are arrrested.

1) Cooperate with arresting officers by providing them with background information and valid identification. This is the only time when it is useful to talk with the cops. If you cannot prove your identity and residence, you will be fingerprinted and placed through the system.

2) Arrive "clean". After an arrest, you will be searched. Posession of weapons or drugs will result in your being put through the system.

3) Commit a relatively minor infraction. Sitting down in the street and refusing to move, blocking the entrance to a building, and related conduct generally is treated by a summons. Resisting arrest by going limp is usually treated by a DAT. Assault and property destruction will normally result in your being put through the system.

4) Have no outstanding warrants. That court date you missed six months ago (Oh shit! That arrest?) has grown into a bench warrant and will result in your being put through the system.

Lying to the police by showing them false identification is stupid and illegal. It is a crime more serious than the one you are trying to get out of. If they take your fingerprints and you have been printed before under another name, you're in trouble.

Sometimes, a lawyer or responsible adult calling or showing up at the precinct can influence the police to release you rather than put you through the system. (That is why your lawyers usually do not stand there during demonstrations and call the police "fucking pigs.")

If the police use summons procedures, you will be taken to a precinct house. A police offficer will ask you background questions. You will then be issued a pink slip of paper with a court date. You will then be released. If you do not show up within 30 days after your date, a warrant will be issued for your arrest. Persons arrested at the same time may be given differenct court dates--a tactic often used to prevent mass demonstrations at the courthouse. Because off the 30-day rule, you have some flexibility in scheduling your court appearance. Like everything else, going to court is more fun with your friends.

If the police put you through the system, you will first go to the precinct for a few hours. From there, you will be taken to Central Booking and fingerprinted. You have no right to refuse these procedures, and you will not be released until they are completed. You will also be interviewed by a representative from "pretrial services". The result of this interview will be used by the judge in determining whether you should be released on your own promise to appear (release on own recognizance, or ROR). It is important to give them the name and telephone number of someone who can verify the information that you provide. Following this process, which may take up to five hours, you will be taken to one of the precincts in Manhattan and held in a small cell for as long as forty-eight hours. They will take your belt and shoelaces away (really!) while you are in the holding cell. Finally, you will be brought to court at 100 Centre Street, where you will wait in the basement in another cell, as long as overnight. You will be brought "upstairs" to yet another cell, where you will wait a bit longer before getting to see a judge. Just before you see the judge, you will see an attorney, either Legal Aid or from your defense committee.

A trip through the system is no fun, but you can do it.

DISCLAIMER: The advice given here is meant as a general statement of the law, and should not substitute your spending a pile of money on a real flesh and blood lawyer.

Organizing Small and Large Protests

Step 1: Set a Goal and Identify Your Audience
It‚Äôs important to identify what you want to accomplish with your protest. Are you trying to raise awareness? Are you trying to change a policy or law? Once you identify the goal, you then must identify your audience. If you‚re trying to raise awareness, then the general public may be your target audience. However, if you‚Äôre trying to change a policy or law, your target audience will be much different.

Step 2: Determine the Forum and Tone of your Protest
It‚Äôs important to determine a medium for your protest, and how the demonstration will proceed. Maybe the Internet would be the best forum for your demonstration. It worked well for those protesting the SOPA legislation. Perhaps your protest is better suited in a park or on a street corner. It depends on your goal.
Also determine the tone of your protest. Are you going to have a silent sit-in, or will your protest be loud and in your face? The tone will vary depending on what you are protesting and your goal.

Step 3: Set the Location, Date and Time of the Protest
Sometimes the location for your protest will be obvious, other times it won‚Äôt. If you are protesting a law, a government building where the law is being drafted would be an ideal location. But if you are protesting a business with many locations, pick the busiest spot. Check with city officials if you are expecting a large crowd.

The date and time will largely depend on your goal. If you are trying to raise awareness among the general public, then the weekend when people are out and about would be the best time. If you are targeting business executives, weekdays would perhaps be most beneficial.

Step 4: Prepare Content for the Protest
Once you have the location, date and time nailed down, it‚Äôs time to start creating content for the demonstration. Make picket signs

and pamphlets to let people know what you are protesting. If your protest is online, create images and videos with embed codes so they can be easily shared. Finally, refer people to a website before, during and after the event, and put the Web address on all protest materials.

Step 5: Promote the Protest
Depending on your budget, there are many ways to promote a demonstration. From billboards to passing out fliers, there is something for everyone. Some low-cost things you can do to promote your protest include writing a press release, contacting the local media, utilizing social media and asking like-minded groups to use their resources to help spread the word.

Step 6: Stay Positive
Don't get discouraged if you're the only one who shows up, ride out the protest solo. You may have hecklers, but it's important not to get caught up in arguing, hate or negativity. Other people observe your behavior, and you want to be respectful to everyone. The biggest mistake you could make is getting discouraged and feeling like what you're doing isn't making a difference. Stick with it. You might not change anyone's mind during the protest, but understand you're planting a seed that could grow.

Whether you,re planning a small local protest, or something more large scale, these basic steps will get you started. Don't let a lack of knowledge stand in the way of voicing your opinion, it's your First Amendment right to protest, don't be afraid to exercise it.

Before your rally

1. Choose a date, time and location.

If your event is targeting a member of Congress, it makes the most

sense to hold your rally outside of their office. If your city has central town square, this can also be a great location. Or maybe it makes sense to pick a location that ties to the issue you're focusing

on. When choosing a location, consider direct pressure on your target, accessibility, parking and visibility -- to the public and the media.

Rallies are often held during business hours (starting no earlier than 8:30 am and no later than 4:30), when we have the best chance of getting media and the attention of Congress. The lunch hour is often the best time during the business day to turn out the most people -- and it's a convenient time for reporters.

If you have an event outside of a member of Congress' office, it's a good idea to call them as soon as you've determined your date and time. It's great to ask if you can meet with their office before or after the event. If you do get a meeting, be sure to review the MoveOn District Meeting guide.

2. Register your event online

Register your event in MoveOn's online system as soon as possible. As long as it meets the criteria for a given action, and is posted by the appropriate deadline, we can send an email to active MoveOn members in your area to invite them to your event. Check with your Council Coordinator, Regional Coordinator or Field Organizer to make sure your event meets the necessary criteria to qualify for a recruitment email.

3. Line up speakers.

Here are a few examples of speakers it may make sense to invite:

Everyday folks with compelling personal stories related to the issue. For example, during a health care campaign, Councils often invited people to speak who had been denied coverage because of pre-existing conditions.

Small business owners

Community leaders

Veterans have a unique role and stature in public policy debates because of their service to our country.

Clergy

Local/State Elected Officials: Mayors, state representatives, state senators, city council members and others in the area. (Note: in an election year, do not to invite anyone who is running for public office.)

It's very important that you prepare your speakers well. Make sure to have a prep call or meeting with everyone who is speaking at your rally.

4. Plan logistics.

Do you need a sound system? If you're in a large city where you've had large crowds in the past, you should arrange to have at least a basic sound system.

Do you need a permit for your event? In most communities, you don't need a permit to stand on public property -- including public sidewalks. But depending on the location of your event, you may want to check with local authorities ahead of time. Many senate offices are in federal buildings that do require permits. If you're unsure, just check with local authorities. Also, if you have a sound system, you are more likely to need to arrange a permit. If you run into any questions or problems, talk to your Regional Coordinator or Field Organizer.

What roles need to be filled? This depends on the size and details of your event, but here are some roles to consider planning for:

Greeter: As the rally host, you'll have a lot to attend to -- so it's good to designate someone specifically to attend to the people who come to your event, greeting them as they arrive, talking with them, making them feel welcome, and signing them in. (Click here for a sign-in sheet.) This is a really important role for getting new folks interested and involved in your Council.

Emcee: This person starts and concludes the rally, introduces speakers, and keeps the program on time. Think of this person as the "master of ceremonies."

Cheer-leader: This person leads chants and cheers at the rally.

Visuals & Sign Coordinator: This person is in charge of coordinating a group of folks who will make or print signs and other visuals for the event.

5. Prepare the materials you'll need

You'll want to make or print signs to hold at your event. Other materials you may want to have on hand include: sign-in sheets, copies of the media advisory, and notes about what you want to say. Check with your Regional Coordinator or Field Organizer to make sure you have all the materials that MoveOn campaigners have produced for the event.

6. Recruit people to your event.

Hit the phones: The most tried-and-true way we know to get people out to events is to pick up the phone and call them. Our call tool makes it easy to call active MoveOn members in your area. Click here for the MoveOn Recruitment Guide.

Emails: You can also invite people over email from your host tools page. Make sure you at least invite every Council member and everyone who recently attended a Council event! Here's how:

To send the invite email, log in to your host tools page. From there, you can easily send invitations using the "Invite Others" tool. (This will automatically add the details of your event and a link to RSVP.)

The personalized link to your host tools page is included in the confirmation email you receive when you post your event online.

7. Contact the media.

It's really important to get the media to cover your event - news coverage educates other constituents on the issue, and puts additional pressure on your target. Click here for the MoveOn Media Guide -- use it to invite members of the media to your event.

8. Have a final check-in call with your group.

Walk through the event from start to finish to make sure everything is ready and everyone is clear about their role. Anyone who is speaking or playing a role should be on the call. You can also discuss any breaking political updates related to the issue.

9. Make final preparations -- including reminder calls

In the last 24 hours before your event, make sure you're ready! Re-read this guide and review all your materials. Also, be sure to check in with any local organizational partners (if applicable) the day before the event to finalize any logistics items and talk through any questions. Then make sure you talk to your Council Coordinator, Regional Coordinator or Field Organizer before the action for final tips and prep.

Your registered guests should hear from you in the 24 hours leading up to the event. This is by far the best way to help ensure that people show up. You should give them a reminder call. If they listed their phone numbers, that information will show up on your host tools page. You should also log in to your host tools page to send an email to everyone who RSVPed, reminding them what time you are starting and how to get there.

During your rally.

Arrive at least 20 minutes early. Typically some folks will show up early, and you'll want to be there to greet them.

If your event is at a Congressional office, the first thing you should

do when you arrive is to go and give the staff a heads-up that you're there. They should know that you're coming, as you will have called them, but this still makes sense as a courtesy.

Welcome people as they arrive, and ask folks to start displaying their signs.

Start as close to on-time as possible. Don't wait more than ten minutes after your advertised start-time -- especially if any reporters are there. Here's a sample 1-hour rally agenda, assuming a start-time of 12:00 noon:

Arrive early -- no later than 11:40am to make sure there are no unanticipated logistical issues, and to greet folks who arrive early.

Starting at 11:45am - Greet reporters as they arrive. You can usually identify reporters as people with notebooks who aren't participating in the rally. TV reporters usually arrive in vans with TV station logos on them and will have large cameras. Radio reporters often have visible recording equipment also. Again, it's best if someone (like your Council's Media Coordintor) is set up to do just this task and nothing else. See the MoveOn Media Guide for more detailed information.

11:45-12:05 - As people arrive, greeters welcome them and sign them in (click here for rally sign-in sheets). You'll want at least one designated greeter -- more if you anticipate more than 40 people.

11:45-12:10 - Lead the crowd in cheers and chants. Again, it's best if someone is set up with a megaphone or other sound system for this

12:10-12:15 - Emcee officially starts the event, thanks people for coming, and briefly states why you're all there. You should let people know how long the rally will go.

12:15-12:20 - First speaker (introduced by emcee)

12:20-12:25 - Second speaker (introduced by emcee)

12:25-12:30 - Third speaker (introduced by emcee)

12:30-12:40 - Emcee wraps up prepared statements and takes questions from the media

12:40-12:50 - Continued chanting and cheering

12:50-12:55 - Emcee thanks people again for coming, repeats any important next step actions people should take, and announces any upcoming MoveOn Council events or meetings.

Organizing protest tips

The public event should take no more than one hour.

Ask others to step up into roles -- don't run a one-person show!

If you are on a public sidewalk, make sure to keep a path clear for passersby.

People often tend to huddle close together -- and this often makes their signs less visible and makes the crowd look smaller. Encourage folks to spread out and to make their signs visible to the public and the media.

Chants are often a great energizer.

After your rally:

1. Hold a meeting to debrief your rally and to talk about next steps. Plan that gathering to take place within 10 days of your rally.

2. Follow-up with folks who attended your rally:

Call through your sign-up sheets to thank people for coming and ask them to attend the debrief/next steps meeting.

Debrief with any members who took on leadership roles during the

event. This includes greeters, the Emcee and other coordinators.

Share any news coverage and press clippings with attendees. (It's also great to send this to the office of your member of Congress.)

Send a thank-you note to any of the speakers from your event.

3. Fill out the survey you'll receive via email after the event. And email any photos from the event.

4. Celebrate, and talk to your Council Coordinator, Regional Coordinator or Field Organizer to get ready for what's next.

How to Organize a March on Washington

1.Start planning at least three months ahead of your anticipated march. Permits are approved within 48 hours but you can submit them up to a year or more in advance. The earlier you start, the better.

2. Contact the National Parks Permit Office by calling (202) 619-7225. Ask them to fax you a permit application.

3.Visit the Dcpages website for a map of the District of Colombia. Determine the protest gathering point, march route and rally area. Print the map by hitting the "Print Screen" button on the keyboard. Use a yellow highlighter to plot out the different protest points on the map.

4.Call the National Parks Permit Office again; Ask them for the availability dates on the gathering location, march route and rally point. Once they have confirmed availability, proceed to fill out the entire application.

5. Make sure to specify the estimated number of people participating in the protest and the main contact person. That person must sign and date the application.

6. Make a copy of the application and the highlighted map for your records.

7. Mail the original application and highlighted map to: National Parks Permit Office, Room 128, 1100 Ohio Drive Southwest, Washington, District of Colombia 20242.

8. Wait about a week for a National Parks Agent to call. This agent will be specifically assigned to your organization for the permit application process. Have the agent give you her direct extension for further questions and information.

9. Provide the agent with any additional information he may need to approve the permit. Ask him to fax you the approved permit immediately and mail the original back to you.

10.Start campaigning for participants with your permit in hand. The National Parks Permit Office will take care of notifying the District of Colombia Police and other city organizations that require special events notification.

BC 470-391
China
Mohism

The Mohist philosophical school disapproved of war. However, since they lived in a time of warring polities, they cultivated the science of fortification. One consequence of Mohist understanding of mathematics and the physical sciences combined with their skills as artisans was that they became the pre-eminent siege engineers during the period prior to the Qin unification China, capable of both reducing defenses and holding cities. The Mohists beliefs were outside the mainstream of Chinese thought and culture; however, because of their utility as siege engineers, they were tolerated and employed for their skills.

In addition to creating a school of philosophy, the Mohists formed a highly structured political organization that tried to realize the ideas they preached. Mohists developed the sciences of fortification and statecraft, and wrote treatises on government, ranging in topic from efficient agricultural production to the laws of inheritance. They were often hired by the many warring kingdoms as advisers to the state.

Around 26-36 AD
Judea
Pontius Pilate

Jews demonstrated in Caesarea to try to convince Pontius Pilate
not to set up Roman standards, with images of the Roman emper-
or and the eagle of Jupiter, in Jerusalem (both images were considered idolatrous by religious Jews). Pilate surrounded the Jewish
protesters with soldiers and threatened them with death, to which
they replied that they were willing to die rather than see the laws of
the Torah violated.

Josephus notes that while Pilate's predecessors had respected
Jewish customs by removing all images and effigies on their standards when entering Jerusalem, Pilate allowed his soldiers to bring
them into the city at night. When the citizens of Jerusalem discov-
ered these the following day, they appealed to Pilate to remove the
ensigns of Caesar from the city. After five days of deliberation,
Pilate had his soldiers surround the demonstrators, threatening
them with death, which they were willing to accept rather than submit to desecration of Mosaic law. Pilate finally removed the images.

Before 1500-1835
Chatham Islands, New Zealand
Moriori

The Moriori were a branch of the New Zealand M_ori that colonized the Chatham Islands and eventually became hunter-gatherers. Their lack of resources and small population made conventional war unsustainable, so it became customary to resolve disputes nonviolently or ritually. Due to this tradition of nonviolence, the entire population of 2000 people was enslaved, killed or cannibalized when 900 M_ori invaded the island in 1835.

On 19 November 1835, the brig Lord Rodney, a hijacked European ship, arrived carrying 500 M_ori armed with guns, clubs and axes, and loaded with 78 tones of seed potatoes, followed by another ship with 400 more M_ori on 5 December 1835. While the second shipment of invaders were waiting, the invaders killed a 12-year-old girl and hung her flesh on posts. They proceeded to enslave some Moriori and kill and cannibalise others.

1756-1920
USA
Women's Suffrage in the United States

A political movement that spanned over a century, where women protested in order to receive the right to suffrage in the United States. Agitation was suspended during the Civil War but resumed in 1865 when the National Woman's Rights Committee issued a petition asking Congress to amend the United States Constitution to prohibit states from disfranchising citizens "on the ground of sex."

Women's suffrage in the United States was achieved gradually, at state and local levels during the late 19th century and early 20th century, culminating in 1920 with the passage of the Nineteenth Amendment to the United States Constitution, which provided: "The right of citizens of the United States to vote shall not be denied or abridged by the United States or by any State on account of sex."

1819
England
Peterloo massacre

Famine and chronic unemployment, coupled with the lack of suffrage in northern England, led to a peaceful demonstration of
60,000-80,000 persons, including women and children. The
demonstration was organized and rehearsed, with a "prohibition of
all weapons of offense or defense" and exhortations to come
"armed with no other weapon but that of a self-approving con-
science". Cavalry charged into the crowd, with sabres drawn, and
in the ensuing confusion, 15 people were killed and 400-700 were
injured. Newspapers expressed horror, and Percy Shelley glorified
nonviolent resistance in the poem The Masque of Anarchy.
However, the British government cracked down on reform, with the
passing of what became known as the Six Acts. The massacre was
given the name Peterloo in an ironic comparison to the Battle of
Waterloo, which had taken place four years earlier.

1834-38
Trinidad
End of Slavery in Trinidad

The United Kingdom of Great Britain and Ireland, then the colonial power in Trinidad, first announced in 1833 the impending total liberation of slaves by 1840. In 1834 at an address by the Governor at Government House about the new laws, an unarmed group of mainly elderly people of African descent began chanting: Pas de six ans. Point de six ans ("Not six years. No six years"), drowning out the voice of the Governor. Peaceful protests continued until the passing of a resolution to abolish apprenticeship and the achievement of de facto freedom.

Peaceful protests continued until a resolution to abolish apprenticeship was passed and de facto freedom was achieved. This may have been partially due to the influence of Dr. Jean Baptiste Phillipe's book, A Free Mulatto (1824).

1838
USA
Cherokee Removal

The Cherokee refused to recognize the fraudulent Treaty of New Echota and therefore did not sell their livestock or goods, and did not pack anything to travel to the west before the soldiers came and forcibly removed them. That ended tragically in the Cherokee Trail of Tears. The phrase "Trail of Tears" originated from a description of the removal of the Choctaw Nation in 1831. The Cherokee Trail of Tears resulted from the enforcement of the Treaty of New Echota, an agreement signed under the provisions of the Indian Removal Act of 1830, which exchanged Native American land in the East for lands west of the Mississippi River, but which was never accepted by the elected tribal leadership or a majority of the Cherokee people.

1849-1867
Habsburg Monarchy
Passive Resistance (Hungary)

In the failed Hungarian Revolution of 1848, the Hungarians tried to regain independence, and were defeated by the Austrian Empire only with the aid of the Russian Empire. After 1848, the empire instituted several constitutional reforms, trying to resolve the problem, but without success. The resistance was instrumental in keeping up hope and spirit in a Hungary fully incorporated into Austria and characterized by reprisals against political dissidents, thousands of treason trials, military governance, centralization, absolutism, censorship and direct control of Vienna over every aspect of public life. Their followers carefully avoided any political agitation or criticism of the establishment, and strictly concentrated on national issues of non-political nature, such as the use of the Hungarian language, development of the Hungarian economy, and protection of the legal standing of the Hungarian Academy of Sciences.

1860-1894, 1915-1918
New Zealand
Tainui-Waikato

Mori King Tawhiao forbade Waikato Mori using violence in the face of British colonization, saying in 1881 "The killing of men must stop; the destruction of land must stop. I shall bury my patu in the earth and it shall not rise again ... Waikato, lie down. Do not allow blood to flow from this time on." This was inspirational to Waikato Mori who refused to fight in World War I. In response, the government brought in conscription for the Tainui-Waikato people, but they continued to resist, the majority of conscripts choosing to suffer harsh military punishments rather than join the army. For the duration of the war, no Tainui soldiers were sent overseas.

1879-1880
New Zealand
Parihaka

The Maori village of Parihaka became the center of passive resist-ance campaigns against Europeans occupying confiscated land in the area. More than 400 followers of the prophet Te Whiti-o-Rongomai were arrested and jailed, most without trial. Sentences as long as 16 months were handed out for the acts of ploughing land and erecting fences on their property. More than 2000 inhabi-tants remained seated when 1600 armed soldiers raided and destroyed the village. North Taranaki Mori, including children, were then separated-"like drafting sheep," one newspaper reported-and then marched under guard to Waitara. To starve out the remainder, soldiers destroyed all surrounding crops, wiping out 45 acres (180,000 m2) of potatoes, taro and tobacco, then began repeating the measure across the countryside.

1908-62
Samoa
Mau movement

Nonviolent movement for Samoan independence from colonial rule in the early 20th century. The word 'Mau' means 'opinion,' 'unwavering,' 'to be decided,' or 'testimony' denoting 'firm strength' in Samoan. The motto for the Mau were the words Samoa mo Samoa (Samoa for the Samoans). The Mau movement culminated on 28 December 1929 in the streets of the capital Apia, when the New Zealand military police fired on a procession who were attempting to prevent the arrest of one of their members. The day became known as Black Saturday. Up to 11 Samoans were killed, including Mau leader and high chief Tupua Tamasese Lealofi III with many others wounded. One New Zealand constable was clubbed to death by protesters.

1919. 2.8, 3.1
Korea
March 1st Movement

This movement became the inspiration of the later Mohandas Karamchand Gandhi's Satyagraha-resistance and many other non-violent movement in Asia. The name refers to an event that occurred on March 1, 1919, hence the movement's name, literally meaning "Three-One Movement" or "March First Movement" in Korean. The Samil Movement came as a result of the repressive nature of colonial occupation under the military rule of the Japanese Empire following 1905, and the "Fourteen Points" outlining the right of national "self-determination" proclaimed by President Woodrow Wilson at the Paris Peace Conference in January 1919. After hearing news of Wilson's speech, Korean students studying in Tokyo published a statement demanding freedom from colonial rule.

Adding to this was the death of former Emperor Kojong on January 21, 1919. There was widespread suspicion that he had been poisoned, credible since previous attempts (the "coffee plot") were well-known.

1919-22
Egypt
Egyptian Revolution of 1919

A countrywide revolution against the British occupation of Egypt. It was carried out by Egyptians from different walks of life in the wake of the British-ordered exile of revolutionary leader Saad Zaghlul and other members of the Wafd Party in 1919. The event led to Egyptian independence in 1922 and the implementation of a new constitution in 1923.

Prior to the war, nationalist agitation was limited to the educated elite. Over the course of the war however, dissatisfaction with the British occupation spread amongst all classes of the population. This was the result of Egypt's increasing involvement in the war, despite Britain's promise to shoulder the entire burden of the war. During the war, the British poured masses of foreign troops into Egypt, conscripted over one and a half million Egyptians into the Labour Corps, and requisitioned buildings, crops, and animals for the use of the army.

1919-21
Ireland
Irish Non-cooperation movement

During the Irish War for Independence, Irish nationalists used many non-violent means to resist British rule. Amongst these was abstention from the British parliament, tax boycotts, and the creation of alternative local government, Dáil Courts, and police.
A policy of ostracism of RIC men was announced by the Dáil on 11 April 1919. This proved successful in demoralizing the force as the war went on, as people turned their faces from a force increasingly compromised by association with British government repression.
The rate of resignation went up, and recruitment in Ireland dropped off dramatically. Often the RIC were reduced to buying food at gunpoint as shops and other businesses refused to deal with them.
Some RIC men cooperated with the IRA through fear or sympathy, supplying the organization with valuable information.

1919-present
Palestine
First Intifada
Second Intifada
Palestinian Protests in West Bank

Palestinian groups have worked with Israelis and foreign citizens to organize civilian monitors of Israeli military activity in the West Bank and Gaza Strip. Peace camps and strategic non-violent resistance to Israeli construction of Jewish settlements and of the West Bank Barrier have also been consistently adopted as tactics by Palestinians. Citizens of the Palestinian village of Beit Sahour also engaged in a tax strike during the First Intifada.

In 2010, A "White Intifada" took hold in the West Bank, including East Jerusalem. Weekly protests by Peaceful Palestinian activities accompanied by B'Tselem (the Israeli Information Center for Human Rights in the Occupied Territories) in addition to Israel academics and students against settlers and security forces. The EU through its foreign policy chief Catherine Ashton has criticized Israel for convicting an organizer of the peaceful movement and said that she was deeply concerned about the arrest of Abdullah Abu Rahmeh. There have been two fatalities among protesters and an American peace activist suffered brain damage after being hit by a tear gas canister.

1920-22
British India
Non-cooperation Movement

A series of nationwide people's movements of nonviolent resistance and civil disobedience, led by Mohandas Karamchand
Gandhi (Mahatma Gandhi) and the Indian National Congress. In
addition to bringing about independence, Gandhi's nonviolence
also helped improve the status of the Untouchables in Indian society. After the Jallianwala Bagh incident, Gandhi started the Non-
Cooperation movement. It aimed to resist British occupation in
India through nonviolent means. Protestors would refuse to buy
British goods, adopt the use of local handicrafts, picket liquor
shops, and try to uphold the Indian values of honor and integrity.
The ideals of Ahimsa and nonviolence, and Gandhi's ability to rally
hundreds of thousands of common citizens towards the cause of
Indian independence, were first seen on a large scale in this move-
ment through the summer 1920, they feared that the movement
might lead to popular nonviolence.

1923
Germany
The Occupation of the Ruhr

With the aim of occupying the centre of German coal, iron, and steel production in the Ruhr valley; France invaded Germany for neglecting some of its reparation payments after World War I. The occupation of the Ruhr was initially greeted by a campaign of passive resistance. Approximately 130 German civilians were killed by the French occupation army during the events. Some theories assert that to pay for passive resistance in the Ruhr, the German government began the hyperinflation that destroyed the German economy in 1923. Others state that the road to hyperinflation was well established before with the reparation payments that started on November 1921. In the face of economic collapse, with high unemployment and hyperinflation, the strikes were eventually called off in September 1923 by the new Gustav Stresemann coalition government, which was followed by a state of emergency.

1930-34
British India
Civil Disobedience Movement

Nonviolent resistance marked by rejecting British imposed taxes, boycotting British manufactured products and mass strikes, led by Mohandas Karamchand Gandhi (Mahatma Gandhi) and the Indian National Congress. The Salt March, also mainly known as the Salt Satyagraha, began with the Dandi March on 12 March 1930, and was an important part of the Indian independence movement. It was a direct action campaign of tax resistance and nonviolent protest against the British salt monopoly in colonial India, and triggered the wider Civil Disobedience Movement. This was the most significant organised challenge to British authority since the Non-cooperation movement of 1920-22, and directly followed the Purna Swaraj declaration of independence by the Indian National Congress on 26 January 1930.

1933-45
Germany
German Resistance

Throughout World War II, there were a series of small and usually isolated groups that used nonviolent techniques against the Nazis. These groups include the White Rose and the Confessional Church. Approximately 77,000 German citizens were killed for one or another form of resistance by Special Courts, courts-martial, People's Court and the civil justice system. Many of these Germans had served in government, the military, or in civil positions, which enabled them to engage in subversion and conspiracy; in addition the Canadian historian Peter Hoffman counts unspecified "tens of thousands" in concentration camps who were either suspected or actually engaged in opposition. The resistance in Germany included German citizens of non-German ethnicity, such as members of the Polish minority who formed resistance groups like Olimp.

1940-43
Denmark
Danish Resistance Movement

During World War II, after the invasion of the Wehrmacht, the Danish government adopted a policy of official co-operation (and unofficial obstruction) which they called "negotiation under protest." Embraced by many Danes, the unofficial resistance included slow production, emphatic celebration of Danish culture and history, and bureaucratic quagmires. Due to the initially lenient arrangements, in which the Nazi occupation authority allowed the democratic government to stay in power, the resistance movement was slower to develop effective tactics on a wide scale than in some other countries.

By 1943, many Danes were involved in underground activities, ranging from producing illegal publications to spying and sabotage. Major groups included the communist BOPA (Danish: Borgerlige Partisaner, Civil Partisans) and Holger Danske, both based in Copenhagen.

1940-45
Norway
Norwegian Resistance Movement

During World War II, Norwegian civil disobedience included preventing the Nazification of Norway's educational system, distributing of illegal newspapers, and maintaining social distance (an "ice front") from the German soldiers. This involved, among other things, never speaking to a German if it could be avoided (many pretended to speak no German, though it was then almost as prevalent as English is now) and refusing to sit beside a German on public transportation. The latter was so annoying to the occupying German authorities that it became illegal to stand on a bus if seats were available.

The first mass outbreak of civil disobedience occurred in the autumn of 1940, when students of Oslo University began to wear paper clips on their lapels to demonstrate their resistance to the German occupiers and their Norwegian collaborators. A seemingly innocuous item, the paper clip was a symbol of solidarity and unity ("we are bound together"), implying resistance.

1942
British India
Quit India Movement

The Quit India Movement (Bharat Chhodo Andolan or the August Movement) was a civil disobedience movement launched in India in August 1942 in response to Mohandas Gandhi's call for immediate independence. The call for determined, but appears in his call to Do or Die, issued on 8 August at the Gowaliar Tank Maidan in Mumbai in 1942.

The British were prepared to act. Almost the entire INC leadership, and not just at the national level, was imprisoned without trial within hours after Gandhi's speech. Most spent the rest of the war in prison and out of contact with the masses. The British had the support of the Viceroy's Council (which had a majority of Indians), of the Muslims, the Communist Party, the princely states, the Imperial and state police, the Indian Army, and the Indian Civil Service.

1945-71
South Africa
Defiance Campaign
Internal Resistance to South African Apartheid

The ANC and allied anti-apartheid groups initially carried out non-violent resistance against pro-racial segregation and apartheid governments in South Africa. Internal resistance to the apartheid system in South Africa came from several sectors of society and saw the creation of organizations dedicated variously to peaceful protests, passive resistance and armed insurrection. It came from both black activists like Steve Biko and Desmond Tutu as well as white activists and a large proportion of Jewish activists like Joe Slovo, Denis Goldberg, Harry Schwarz and Helen Suzman. By the 1980s there was continuous interplay between violent and non-violent action, and this interplay was a notable feature of the rebellion against apartheid from 1983 until South Africa's transition to democracy in 1994.

1946-1958
Territory of Hawaii
Hawaii Democratic Revolution of 1954

Following World War II, general strikes were initiated by the large working poor against racial and economic inequality under Hawaii's plantation economy. Movement members took over most of the government in 1954 and the State of Hawaii was established in 1959. The Revolution culminated in the territorial elections of 1954 where the reign of the Hawaii Republican Party in the legislature came to an abrupt end, as they were voted out of office to be replaced by members of the Democratic Party of Hawaii. The strikes by the Isles' labor workers demanded similar pay and benefits to their Mainland counterparts. The strikes also crippled the power of the sugar plantations and the Big Five Oligopoly over their workers.

1955-68
USA
African-American Civil Rights Movement
Chicano Civil Rights Movement
Mass Anti-war Protests in the United States

Tactics of nonviolent resistance, such as bus boycotts, freedom rides, sit-ins, marches, and mass demonstrations, were used during the African American Civil Rights Movement. This movement succeeded in bringing about legislative change, making separate seats, drinking fountains, and schools for African Americans illegal, and obtaining full Voting Rights and open housing.

While most popular representations of the movement are centered around the leadership and philosophy of Martin Luther King Jr., many scholars note that the movement was far too diverse to be credited to one person, organization, or strategy. Churches, local grassroots organizations, fraternal societies, and black-owned businesses mobilized volunteers to participate in broad-based actions. This was a more direct and potentially more rapid means of creating change than the traditional approach of mounting court challenges used by the NAACP and others.

1957-present
USA
Committee for Non-Violent Action

Among the most dedicated to nonviolent resistance against the US arsenal of nuclear weapons has been the Plowshares Movement, consisting largely of Catholic priests, such as Dan Berrigan, and nuns. Since the first Plowshares action in King of Prussia, Pennsylvania during the autumn of 1980, more than 70 of these actions have taken place.

The Committee for Non-Violent Action (CNVA), formed in 1957 to resist the US government's program of nuclear weapons testing, was one of the first organizations to employ nonviolent direct action to protest against the nuclear arms race. The CNVA's immediate antecedent, a committee known as Non-Violent Action Against Nuclear Weapons, was formed by radical Quaker Lawrence Scott.

While never a mass-membership organization, the CNVA's pioneering use of nonviolent direct action would have a significant influence on movements to follow.

1959-present
Cuba
Cuban Opposition since 1959

There have been many nonviolent activists in opposition to Cuba's authoritarian regime. Among these are Pedro Luis Boitel (1931-1972), Guillermo Fariñas Hernández ("El Coco"), and Jorge Luis García Pérez (known as Antúnez), all of whom have performed hunger strikes. There are a number of opposition parties and groups that campaign for political change in Cuba.

Thousands of Cubans protested in Havana and chanted "Libertad!" ("Freedom") during the Maleconazo uprising on August 5, 1994. The uprising lasted a few hours before it was dispersed by the government's security forces, and an intervention by Fidel Castro himself. A paper published in the Journal of Democracy states that this was the closest that the Cuban opposition could come to asserting itself decisively.

1965-1972
USA
Draft resistance

During the Vietnam War, many young Americans chose to resist the military draft by refusing to cooperate with the Selective Service System. Techniques of resistance included misrepresenting one's physical or mental condition to the draft board, disrupting draft board processes, going "underground", going to jail, leaving the country, and publicly promoting such activities.

Members of the Resistance movement publicly burned their draft cards or refused to register for the draft. Other members deposited their cards into boxes on selected dates and then mailed them to the government. They were then drafted, refused to be inducted, and fought their cases in the federal courts. These draft resisters hoped that their public civil disobedience would help to bring the war and the draft to an end. Many young men went to federal prison as part of this movement.

February 11, 1967
USA
Los Angeles Black Cat Protest

Homosexual Bar and Site of Civil Resistance to Heightened Los Angeles Police Department (LAPD) Raids against Homosexual Establishments throughout the City, especially in the Homosexual Quarter known as Sunset Junction(2) District/East Hollywood An Historic Cultural Monument, City of Los Angeles, recognized as a site of Peaceful Civil Resistance in the struggle for Homosexual Civil Rights in the United States. The standoff is significant in that it occurred a year prior to the 1968 Stonewall Riots in New York. The Stonewall Bar in the Greenwich Village section of Manhattan was listed to the National Register of Historic Places in 2001.

A tense standoff and potential riot between Hundreds of LAPD riot gear-laden police officers, who were determined to quell the swelling crowds that exceeded four hundred homosexual citizens, was averted after a last minute plea from then new Governor Ronald Reagan, via an openly gay Republican Judicial Appointee who acted as a personal envoy of the Governor to LAPD Commanders at the site of the standoff, was accepted, and a stand down order given which ordered the hundreds of LAPD officers present to cease and desist from further unprovoked harassment of homosexuals in Los Angeles for decades. The plea was successfully communicated and accepted by the LAPD hierarchy, and represented the first time that a stand down order was given by the LAPD, and was the last time until 2001, that the Los Angeles Police Department would engage in raiding an establishment, or public assembly of homosexuals in Los Angeles for decades. The hundreds who gathered to peacefully protest raids perceived as unwarranted, and often violent, against LGBT meeting sites in Los Angeles, observed a success in the struggle for Homosexual Civil Rights.

1968
Worldwide
Protests of 1968

The protests that raged throughout 1968 were for the most part student-led. Worldwide, campuses became the front-line battle grounds for social change. While opposition to the Vietnam War dominated the protests, students also protested for civil liberties, against racism, for feminism, and the beginnings of the Ecology movement can be traced to the protests against nuclear and biological weapons during this year.

As the waves of protests coming along the 1960s intensified to a new high in 1968, repressive governments through widespread police crack downs, shootings, executions and even massacres marked social conflicts in Mexico, Brazil, Spain, Poland, Czechoslovakia, and China. In West Berlin, Rome, London, Paris, Italy, many American cities, and Argentina, labor unions and students played major roles and also suffered political repression.

1968
Czechoslovakia
Prague Spring

During the 1968 Warsaw Pact invasion of Czechoslovakia, the Czechoslovak citizens responded to the attack on their sovereignty with passive resistance. Russian troops were frustrated as street signs were painted over, their water supplies mysteriously shut off, and buildings decorated with flowers, flags, and slogans like, "An elephant cannot swallow a hedgehog."

The generalized resistance caused the Soviet Union to abandon its original plan to oust the First Secretary. Dubek, who had been arrested on the night of 20 August was taken to Moscow for negotiations. There, he and several other leaders signed, under heavy psychological pressure from Soviet politicians, the Moscow Protocol and it was agreed that Dubek would remain in office and a program of moderate reform would continue.

1970-81
France
Larzac

In response to an expansion of a military base, local farmers including José Bové and other supporters including Lanza del Vasto took part in nonviolent resistance. The military expansion was canceled after ten years of resistance. French syndicalist and peasant activist José Bové moved there during this period in support of the protests. Communards from the nearby Community of the Ark, led by the pacifist Lanza del Vasto, were also very active in opposition to the camp. The workers of the occupied and self-managed Lip factory also took part in the movement.

Because of its history it was chosen as the site of a massive meeting against the World Trade Organization which took place in August 2003. José Bové currently resides in Larzac - he secured nearly 500,000 votes in the 2007 presidential elections.

1979
Iran
Iranian Revolution

The Iranian Revolution of 1979 or 1979 Revolution (often known as the Islamic Revolution), refers to events involving the overthrow of Iran's monarchy under Shah Mohammad Reza Pahlavi. The revolution was unusual for the surprise it created throughout the world: it lacked many of the customary causes of revolution (defeat at war, a financial crisis, peasant rebellion, or disgruntled military), occurred in a nation that was enjoying relatively good material wealth and prosperity, produced profound change at great speed, was massively popular, resulted in the exile of many Iranians, and replaced a pro-Western semi-absolute monarchy with an anti-Western authoritarian theocracy based on the concept of Guardianship of the Islamic Jurists (or velayat-e faqih). It was a relatively non-violent revolution, and helped to redefine the meaning and practice of modern revolutions (although there was violence in its aftermath).

1980-1981
Poland
Solidarity, Solidarnosc Walczaca, Orange Alternative,Movement

Solidarity, a broad anti-communist social movement ranging from people associated with the Roman Catholic Church workers and intellectuals to members of the anti-communist Left (minority), advocated non-violence in its members' activities. Additionally, the Orange Alternative offered a wider group of citizens an alternative way of opposition against the authoritarian regime by means of a peaceful protest that used absurd and nonsensical elements.

By doing this, Orange Alternative participants could not be arrested by the police for opposition to the regime without the authorities becoming a laughing stock. Orange Alternative has been viewed as part of the broader Solidarity movement. Academics Dennis Bos and Marjolein 't Hart have asserted it was the most effective of all Solidarity's factions in bringing about the movement's success.

1986
Philippines
People Power Revolution

A series of nonviolent and prayerful mass street demonstrations that toppled Ferdinand Marcos and placed Corazon C. Aquino into power. After an election which had been condemned by the Catholic Bishops' Conference of the Philippines, over two million Filipinos protested human rights violations, election fraud, massive political corruption, and other abuses of the Marcos regime. Yellow was a predominant theme, the colour being associated with Corazon Aquino and her husband, Benigno S. Aquino, Jr., who was assassinated three years prior.

The majority of the demonstrations took place on a long stretch of Epifanio de los Santos Avenue, more commonly known by its acronym EDSA, in Metropolitan Manila from February 22-25, 1986, and involved over two million Filipino civilians, as well as several political, military, and including religious groups led by Cardinal Jaime Sin, the Archbishop of Manila.

1987-90
The Baltic States (Lithuania, Latvia, Estonia)
Singing Revolution

A cycle of mass demonstrations featuring spontaneous singing in The Baltic States. The movement eventually collected 4,000,000 people who sang national songs and hymns, which were strictly forbidden during the years of the Soviet occupation of the Baltic States, as local rock musicians played. In later years, people acted as human shields to protect radio and TV stations from the Soviet tanks, eventually regaining Lithuania's, Latvia's, and Estonia's independence without any bloodshed.

Massive demonstrations against the Soviet regime began after widespread liberalization of the regime failed to take into account national sensitivities. It was hoped by Moscow that the non-Russian nations would remain within the USSR despite the removal of restrictions on freedom of speech and national icons (such as the local pre-1940 flags).

1989
China
Tiananmen Square protests of 1989

The Tiananmen Square protests of 1989, commonly known as the June Fourth Incident or more accurately '89 Democracy Movement in Chinese, were student-led popular demonstrations in Beijing which took place in the spring of 1989 and received broad support from city residents, exposing deep splits within China's political leadership. The protests were forcibly suppressed by hardline leaders who ordered the military to enforce martial law in the country's capital. The crackdown that initiated on June 3-4 became known as the Tiananmen Square Massacre or the June 4 Massacre as troops with assault rifles and tanks inflicted casualties on unarmed civilians trying to block the military's advance towards Tiananmen Square in the heart of Beijing, which student demonstrators had occupied for seven weeks.

1989
Czechoslovakia
Velvet Revolution

The Velvet Revolution (Czech: sametová revoluce) or Gentle Revolution was a non-violent transition of power in what was then Czechoslovakia. The period of upheaval and transition took place from November 16/17 to December 29, 1989. Popular demonstrations against the one-party government of the Communist Party of Czechoslovakia combined students and older dissidents. The final result was the end of 41 years of Communist rule in Czechoslovakia, and the subsequent conversion to a parliamentary republic.

The term Velvet Revolution was coined by Rita Klímová, the dissidents' English translator who later became the ambassador to the United States. The term was used internationally to describe the revolution, although the Czechs also used the term internally. After the dissolution of Czechoslovakia in 1993, Slovakia used the term Gentle Revolution, the term that Slovaks used for the revolution from the beginning.

1989-90
East Germany
Monday demonstrations in East Germany

The Monday demonstrations in East Germany in 1989 and 1990 (German: Montagsdemonstrationen) were a series of peaceful political protests against the authoritarian government of the German Democratic Republic (GDR) of East Germany that took place every Monday evening.

In Leipzig the demonstrations began on 4 September 1989 after the weekly Friedensgebet (prayer for peace) in the Nikolaikirche with parson Christian Führer, and eventually filled the nearby downtown Karl Marx Square (today known again as Augustusplatz). Safe in the knowledge that the Lutheran Church supported their resistance, many dissatisfied East German citizens gathered in the court of the church, and non-violent demonstrations began in order to demand rights such as the freedom to travel to foreign countries and to elect a democratic government.

1990-91
Azerbaijan SSR
Black January

A crackdown of Azeri protest demonstrations by the Red Army in Baku, Azerbaijan SSR. The demonstrators protested against ethnic violence, demanded the ousting of communist officials and called for independence from the Soviet Union. Black January (Azerbaijani: Qara Yanvar), also known as Black Saturday or the January Massacre, was a violent crackdown in Baku on January 19-20, 1990, pursuant to a state of emergency during the dissolution of the Soviet Union to stop pogroms and violence against the Armenian population in Baku.

In a resolution of January 22, 1990, the Supreme Soviet of Azerbaijan SSR declared that the decree of the Presidium of the Supreme Soviet of the USSR of January 19, used to impose emergency rule in Baku and military deployment, constituted an act of aggression.

2000
Serbia
Otpor!

Otpor! (English: Resistance!) was a civic youth movement that existed as such from 1998 until 2003 in Serbia (then a federal unit within FR Yugoslavia), employing nonviolent struggle against the regime of Slobodan as their course of action. In the course of two-year nonviolent struggle against Milosevic, Otpor spread across Serbia and attracted more than 70,000 supporters. They were credited for their role in the successful overthrow of Slobodan Milo_evi_ on 5 October 2000.

Initially after the overthrow, Otpor! envisioned its role to be that of a political watchdog organization in Serbia. It launched campaigns to hold the new government accountable, pressing for democratic reforms and fighting corruption, as well as insisting on cooperation with the International Criminal Tribunal (ICTY) at the Hague.

2003
Liberia
Women of Liberia Mass Action for Peace

This peace movement, started by women praying and singing in a fish market, brought an end to the Second Liberian Civil War in 2003. A delegation of Liberian women went to Ghana to continue to apply pressure on the warring factions during the peace process. They staged a sit in outside of the Presidential Palace, blocking all the doors and windows and preventing anyone from leaving the peace talks without a resolution. The women of Liberia became a political force against violence and against their government. Their actions brought about an agreement during the stalled peace talks. As a result, the women were able to achieve peace in Liberia after a 14-year civil war and later helped bring to power the country's first female head of state, Ellen Johnson Sirleaf.

2004-05
Israel

Protesters opposing Israel's unilateral disengagement plan of 2004 nonviolently resisted impending evacuations of Jewish settlements in the Gaza Strip and the West Bank. Protesters blocked several traffic intersections, resulting in massive gridlock and delays throughout Israel. While Israeli police had received advance notice of the action, opening traffic intersections proved extremely difficult. Eventually, over 400 demonstrators were arrested, including many juveniles. Further large demonstrations planned to commence when Israeli authorities, preparing for disengagement, cut off access to the Gaza Strip. During the confrontation, mass civil disobedience failed to emerge in Israel proper. However, some settlers and their supporters resisted evacuation non-violently.

Those Israeli citizens who refused to accept government compensation packages and voluntarily vacate their homes prior to the August 15, 2005 deadline, were evicted by Israeli security forces over a period of several days.

2004-2005
Ukraine
Orange Revolution

A series of protests and political events that took place in Ukraine in the immediate aftermath of the run-off vote of the 2004 Ukrainian presidential election which was marred by massive corruption, voter intimidation and direct electoral fraud. Nationwide, the democratic revolution was highlighted by a series of acts of civil disobedience, sit-ins, and general strikes organized by the opposition movement.

The nationwide protests succeeded when the results of the original run-off were annulled, and a revote was ordered by Ukraine's Supreme Court for 26 December 2004. Under intense scrutiny by domestic and international observers, the second run-off was declared to be "fair and free". The final results showed a clear victory for Yushchenko, who received about 52% of the vote, compared to Yanukovych's 44%. Yushchenko was declared the official winner and with his inauguration on 23 January 2005 in Kiev, the Orange Revolution ended.

2005
Lebanon
Cedar Revolution

A chain of demonstrations in Lebanon (especially in the capital Beirut) triggered by the assassination of the former Lebanese Prime Minister Rafik Hariri on February 14, 2005.

The primary goals of the original activists were the withdrawal of Syrian troops from Lebanon and the replacement of a government heavily influenced by Syrian interests with more independent leadership, the establishment of an international commission to investigate the assassination of Prime Minister Hariri, the resignation of security officials to ensure the success of the plan, and the organization of free parliamentary elections. The demonstrators demanded the end of the Syrian influence in Lebanese politics. At the start of the demonstrations, Syria had been maintaining a force of roughly 14,000 soldiers and intelligence agents in Lebanon. Following the demonstrations, the Syrian troops completely withdrew from Lebanon on 27 April 2005.

2010-2011
Tunisia
Tunisian Revolution

A chain of demonstrations against unemployment and government corruption in Tunisia began in December 2010. Protests were triggered by the self-immolation of vegetable seller Mohamed Bouazizi and resulted in the overthrow of 24-year-ruling president Zine el-Abidine Ben Ali on January 14, 2011. The demonstrations were precipitated by high unemployment, food inflation, corruption, a lack of freedom of speech and other political freedoms and poor living conditions.

Following further public protests, Ghannouchi himself resigned on 27 February, and Beji Caid el Sebsi became Prime Minister; two other members of the Interim Government resigned on the following day. On 3 March 2011, the president announced the elections for the Constituent Assembly, which were held on 23 October 2011 with the Islamist Ennahda Party winning the plurality of seats.

2011
Egypt
Egyptian Revolution

A chain of protests, sit-ins, and strikes by millions of Egyptians starting January 25, 2011 eventually led to the resignation of President Hosni Mubarak on February 11. Millions of protesters from a range of socio-economic and religious backgrounds demanded the overthrow of Egyptian President Hosni Mubarak. The revolution included Islamic, liberal, anti-capitalist, nationalist and feminist elements.

The Egyptian protesters' grievances focused on legal and political issues, including police brutality, state-of-emergency laws, lack of free elections and freedom of speech, corruption, and economic issues including high unemployment, food-price inflation and low wages. The protesters' primary demands were the end of the Mubarak regime and emergency law, freedom, justice, a responsive non-military government and a voice in managing Egypt's resources. Strikes by labour unions added to the pressure on government officials.

2011
Syria
Syrian Uprising

Protests against the regime of President Bashar al-Assad began on March 15, 2011. Security forces responded with a harsh crackdown, arresting thousands of dissidents and killing hundreds of protesters. Peaceful protests were largely crushed by the army or subsided as rebels and Islamist fighters took up arms against the government, leading to a full-blown rebellion against the Assad regime.

The first instance of armed insurrection occurred on 4 June 2011 in Jisr ash-Shugur, a city near the Turkish border in Idlib province. Clashes between protesters and security forces continued in the following days. On 6 June, Sunni militiamen and army defectors ambushed a group of security forces heading to the city which was met by a large government counterattack. Fearing a massacre, insurgents and defectors, along with 10,000 residents, fled across the Turkish border.

2011-present
Bahrain
Bahraini uprising (2011-present)

Inspired by the regional Arab Spring, protests started in Bahrain on 14 February. The government responded harshly, killing four protesters camping in Pearl Roundabout. Later, protesters were allowed to reoccupy the roundabout where they staged large marches amounting to 150,000 participants.

On 14 March, Saudi-led GCC forces were requested by the government and entered the country, which the opposition called an "occupation". The following day, a state of emergency was declared and protests paused after a brutal crackdown was launched against protesters, including doctors and bloggers. Nearly 3,000 people have been arrested, and at least five people died due to torture while in police custody. Protests resumed after lifting emergency law on 1 June, and several large rallies were staged by the opposition parties, including a march on 9 March 2012 attended by over 100,000. Smaller-scale protests and clashes outside of the capital have continued to occur almost daily. More than 80 people had died since the start of the uprising.

2011-present
Spain
2011-2013 Spanish protests

The 2011-present Spanish protests, also referred to as the 15-M Movement (Spanish: Movimiento 15-M), the Indignants Movement, and Take the Square #spanishrevolution, are a series of ongoing demonstrations in Spain whose origin can be traced to social networks such as Real Democracy NOW (Spanish: Democracia Real YA) or Youth Without a Future (Spanish: Juventud Sin Futuro), among other civilian digital platforms and 200 other small associations. The protests started on May 15, 2011, with an initial call in 58 Spanish cities.

Even though protesters form a heterogeneous and ambiguous group, they share a strong rejection of unemployment, welfare cuts, Spanish politicians, and the current two-party system in Spain between the Spanish Socialist Workers' Party and the People's Party. Their sentiments also encompass the rejection of the current political system, capitalism, banks and political corruption. Many call for basic rights, which consist of home, work, culture, health and education rights.

2011
USA
Occupy Wall Street

Occupy Wall Street (OWS) is the name given to a protest movement that began on September 17, 2011, in Zuccotti Park, located in New York City's Wall Street financial district, receiving global attention and spawning the Occupy movement against social and economic inequality worldwide.

The Canadian, anti-consumerist, pro-environment group/magazine Adbusters initiated the call for a protest.

The main issues raised by Occupy Wall Street were social and economic inequality, greed, corruption and the perceived undue influence of corporations on government-particularly from the financial services sector. The OWS slogan, "We are the 99%", refers to income inequality and wealth distribution in the U.S. between the wealthiest 1% and the rest of the population. To achieve their goals, protesters acted on consensus-based decisions made in general assemblies which emphasized direct action over petitioning authorities for redress.

2012-present
Mexico
Yo Soy 132

Yo Soy 132 is a social movement composed for the most part of Mexican university students from private and public universities, residents of Mexico, claiming supporters from about 50 cities around the world. It began as opposition to the Institutional Revolutionary Party (PRI) candidate Enrique Peña Nieto and the Mexican media's allegedly biased coverage of the 2012 general election. The name Yo Soy 132, Spanish for "I Am 132", originated in an expression of solidarity with the protest's initiators. The phrase drew inspiration from the Occupy movement and the Spanish 15-M movement.The protest movement was self-proclaimed as the "Mexican spring" (an allusion to the Arab Spring) by its first spokespersons, and called the "Mexican occupy movement" in the international press.

2013-present
Turkey
2013 protests in Turkey

Peaceful protests against reconstruction of Gezi Park at Istanbul's landmark Taksim Square, turned into protests against Turkish Prime Minister Recep Tayyip Erdogan. Over one million people nonviolently resisted police brutal force. Started in Istanbul, protests spread in 10 days to over 82 cities of Turkey. Significant violence from the police side was manifested by use of tear gas and rubber bullets. Many people were arrested, including haphazard arrests of people simply standing at the square.

With no centralised leadership beyond the small assembly that organized the original environmental protest, the protests have been compared to the Occupy movement and the May 1968 events. Social media played a key part in the protests, not least because much of the Turkish media downplayed the protests, particularly in the early stages.

2013-2014
Ukraine
Euromaidan

Protests against President Viktor Yanukovych's decision to sign a trade agreement with Russia began in November 2013. The protests later evolved into a civil uprising demanding Yanukovych's ouster. A crackdown by the Ukrainian police drew condemnation of Yanukovych from the European Union and the United States. On February 23, 2014, protesters seized control of Kiev, forcing Yanukovych to flee to Russia. Parliament later agreed to impeach Yanukovych for his role in the police crackdown.

Despite the impeachment of Yanukovych, the installation of a new government, and the signature of the political provisions of the Ukraine-EU Association Agreement, the protests have been ongoing to sustain pressure on the government, counter pro-Russian protests, and reject Russian occupation of Ukraine. The general area of the pro-Ukraine and pro-Europe protests has shifted from Kiev and western Ukraine to include the eastern and southern areas of the country as well.

2013-present
Ukraine
Do not buy Russian goods!

A campaign to boycott Russian goods as a reaction to a series of Russian trade embargos against Ukraine and military invasion of Russia in Ukraine. The protest started on August 14, 2013 as a reaction to a Russian Federation trade embargo against Ukraine. It was organized by Vidsich on social media. The campaign expanded to mass distribution of leaflets, posters, and stickers in over 45 cities and towns.

Sales of Russian goods in Ukraine decreased by 35-50% in the spring of 2014. In May 2014, Ukrainian supermarkets began to abandon the procurement of Russian goods. Delivery of goods from Russia fell by a third. From January to May 2014, according to Standard & Poor's ratings, banks with Russian capital in Ukraine lost more than 50% of deposits.

1957, May 17
Prayer Pilgrimage for Freedom

First large demonstration of the African-American civil rights movement in Washington. Martin Luther King, Jr. demands "Give us the ballot"!

The demonstration was planned at the occasion of the third anniversary of the Brown vs. Board of Education, a landmark Supreme Court decision against segregation in public schools. The event organizers urged the government to abide by that decision, as the process of desegregation was being obstructed at local and state levels.

The march was organized by A. Philip Randolph and Bayard Rustin, and was supported by the NAACP and the recently founded Southern Christian Leadership Conference. Congressman Adam Clayton Powell Jr. had asked the planners not to embarrass the Eisenhower administration, thus the event was organized as a prayer commemoration.

1963, August 28
March on Washington for Jobs and Freedom.

Major civil rights march at which Martin Luther King, Jr. delivered his "I Have a Dream" speech from the steps of the Lincoln Memorial. 250,000 march.

A. Phillip Randolph and Bayard Rustin began planning the march in December 1962. They envisioned two days of protest, including sit-ins and lobbying followed by a mass rally at the Lincoln Memorial. They wanted to focus on joblessness and to call for a public works program that would employ blacks. In early 1963 they called publicly for "a massive March on Washington for jobs". They received help from Amalgamated Clothing Workers unionist Stanley Aronowitz, who gathered support from radical organizers who could be trusted not to report their plans to the Kennedy administration. The unionists offered tentative support for a march that would be focused on jobs.

1965, November 27
March on Washington for Peace in Vietnam

Organized by the Committee for a Sane Nuclear Policy (SANE). An estimated 20,000 to 35,000 attended. SANE's political director Sanford Gottlieb was the march chairman. The National Coordinating Committee to End the War in Vietnam, the SDS, and Women Strike for Peace were also involved.

SANE's Norman Cousins acted as an unofficial liaison between President Kennedy and Soviet Premier Nikita Khrushchev on the Partial Test Ban Treaty negotiations. The organization helped secure the passage of the War Powers Resolution. As the Vietnam War began to escalate, SANE organized a rally at Madison Square Garden that attracted 18,000 people opposing the war, as well as a march on Washington in November 1965 drawing 35,000. Three days after the march, Vice-president Hubert Humphrey met with SANE leaders Dr. Spock, Sanford Gottlieb, and Homer Jack "to openly, responsibly, and frankly discuss their proposals" to end the war. Many more SANE marches on Washington would occur throughout the war.

1967, October 21
March on the Pentagon
National Mobilization

Committee to End the War in Vietnam sponsored the Saturday march to protest the Vietnam War. Around 50,000 railed at the Lincoln Memorial in the morning for speeches and songs, although not all continued across the Arlington Memorial Bridge to the Pentagon. Organizers claimed 100,000 or more marches, but two intelligence agencies and an analysis of aerial reconnaissance photographs from a Navy Skywarrior plane estimated 35,000.

A simultaneous march in San Francisco was attended by Coretta Scott King. At the New York march its last speaker, James Bevel, the Spring Mobilization's chairman and initiator of the march on the U.N. (until Bevel came aboard at the invitation of A.J. Muste and David Dellinger the plan was for just an April 15 rally in Central Park), made an impromptu announcement that the next major anti-war gathering would be in Washington D.C.

1968, January 15
Jeannette Rankin Brigade

A group of women's pro-peace organizations, including the Women's International League for Peace and Freedom and Women Strike for Peace, joined together as to confront Congress on its opening day, January 15, 1968, with a strong show of female opposition to the Vietnam War." At age 87, Jeannette Rankin led the march of some 5,000 women.

The Women's International League for Peace and Freedom (WILPF) developed out of an International Women's Congress against World War I that took place in The Hague, the Netherlands,in 1915, although the name WILPF was not chosen until 1919. It is a non-profit non-governmental organization working "to bring together women of different political views and philosophical and religious backgrounds determined to study and make known the causes of war and work for a permanent peace" and to unite women worldwide who oppose oppression and exploitation.

1968, May 12 - June 19
Poor People's Campaign

SCLC campaign to push for a Federal $30 billion anti-poverty package. Several thousand demonstrators built and camped in Resurrection City, while they lobbied Congress for the program. It was organized by Martin Luther King, Jr. and the Southern Christian Leadership Conference, and carried out in the wake of King's assassination.

After presenting an organized set of demands to Congress and executive agencies, participants set up a 3000-person tent city on the Washington Mall, where they stayed for six weeks. Dr. King wanted to bring poor people to Washington D.C., forcing politicians to see them and think about their needs: "We ought to come in mule carts, in old trucks, any kind of transportation people can get their hands on. People ought to come to Washington, sit down if necessary in the middle of the street and say, 'We are here; we are poor; we don't have any money; you have made us this way...and we've come to stay until you do something about it.'"

1969, October 15
Moratorium to End the War in Vietnam

Vietnam Moratorium. 200,000 demonstrate against the Vietnam War. The Moratorium to End the War in Vietnam was a massive demonstration and teach-in against the United States involvement in the Vietnam War that took place across the United States on October 15, 1969, followed a month later by a large Moratorium March on Washington.

As with previous large anti-war demonstrations, including the National Mobilization Committee to End the War in Vietnam's April 15, 1967 march on the United Nations and their 1967 March on the Pentagon, the event was a clear success, with millions participating throughout the world. Boston was the site of the largest turnout; about 100,000 attended a speech by anti-war Senator George McGovern. Future U.S. President Bill Clinton, then a Rhodes Scholar at Oxford, organized and participated in the demonstration in England; this later became an issue in his Presidential campaign.

1969, November 15
National Mobilization Committee to End the War in Vietnam

Vietnam Moratorium, 600,000 demonstrate against the war in Vietnam. The Spring Mobilization Committee to End the War in Vietnam, which became the National Mobilization Committee to End the War in Vietnam, was a coalition of antiwar activists fo rmed in 1967 to organize large demonstrations in opposition to the Vietnam War. The organizations were info rmally known as "the Mobe".

The first nationwide Moratorium was followed a month later, on Saturday, November 15, 1969, by a second massive Moratorium march in Washington, D.C., which attracted over 500,000 demonstrators against the war, including many performers and activists. This massive Saturday march and rally was preceded by the March against Death, which began on Thursday evening and continued throughout that night and all the next day. Over 40,000 people gathered to parade silently down Pennsylvania Avenue to the White House.

1970, April 4
Victory March

A rally, organized by the Reverend Carl McIntire, the fundamentalist preacher and anticommunist radio commentator, calling for victory in the Vietnam War. The rally drew 50,000 protesters.

Carl McIntire (May 17, 1906 - March 19, 2002) was a founder and minister in the Bible Presbyterian Church, founder and long president of the International Council of Christian Churches and the American Council of Christian Churches, and a popular religious radio broadcaster, who proudly identified himself as a fundamentalist. McIntire also gained the public eye in the early 1970s when he organized a half dozen pro-Vietnam War "Victory Marches" in Washington, D.C.

1970, May 9
Kent State/Cambodian Incursion Protest

A week after the Kent State shootings, 100,000 demonstrators converged on Washington to protest the shootings and President Richard Nixon's incursion into Cambodia.

The Cambodian Campaign (also known as the Cambodian Incursion and the Cambodian Invasion) was a series of military operations conducted in eastern Cambodia during mid-1970 by the United States and the Republic of Vietnam (South Vietnam) during the Vietnam War. These invasions were a result of the policy of President Richard Nixon. A total of 13 major operations were conducted by the Army of the Republic of Vietnam (ARVN) between 29 April and 22 July and by US forces between 1 May and 30 June.

1970, July 4
Honor America Day

A rally put together by supporters of President Nixon. Billy Graham gave the keynote address:

"But I want to tell you it's tremendously heartening to see these thousands of people from all over the country, and it proves one thing, the railroads are still running. And we have telegrams from thousands of others who wished they could be with us, but they are still stacked up over the airport. That's one nice thing about America, you can get a crowd like this together even without a football game, and what a gathering. President Nixon saw this crowd and said 'My God, what did Agnew say now.' And Spiro looked out of his window, saw this crowd and said, 'My God, what a great time to say something.'"

1970, August 26
Women's Strike for Equality

Held nation-wide, it brought out around 20,000 female protestors in D.C. , New York City elsewhere to demand equal rights for women. The march helped expand the women's movement

The Women's Strike for Equality was a strike which took place in the United States on August 26, 1970. It celebrated the 50th anniversary of the passing of the Nineteenth Amendment, which effectively gave American women the right to vote. The rally was sponsored by the National Organization for Women (NOW). More than 20,000 women gathered for the protest in New York City and throughout the country. At this time, the gathering was the largest on behalf of women in the United States. The strike primarily focused on equal opportunity in the workforce, political rights for women, and social equality in relationships such as marriage.

1971, April 19-23
Operation Dewey Canyon III

Sponsored by the Vietnam Veterans Against the War and named after Operation Dewey Canyon, this anti-Vietnam War march included over 1,000 veterans camping on the National Mall and protests all over the city. John Kerry testifies in front of Senate.

This peaceful anti-war protest organized by VVAW took its name from two short military invasions of Laos by US and South Vietnamese forces. Dubbed "Operation Dewey Canyon III," it took place in Washington, D.C, April 19 through April 23, 1971. It was referred to by the participants as "a limited incursion into the country of Congress." The level of media publicity and Vietnam veteran participation at the Dewey Canyon week of protest events far exceeded the Winter Soldier Investigation and any previous VVAW protest event.

.

1971, April 24
Vietnam War Out Now rally

A peaceful Vietnam War Out Now rally on the National Mall, Washington, D.C., with 200,000 calling for an end to the Vietnam War. The march passed the White House, with people carrying names of soldiers and other Americans who had died in Vietnam. Referred to as the March Against Death, this was the beginning of the rally, which culminated in a march.

The non-violent protest took place in downtown Washington, D.C., with protesters marching along Pennsylvania Avenue. The protesters also held a rally at the Washington Monument. After the main demonstration, some radical activists burned an American flag and hurled paint bombs at the Labor and Justice Department buildings. Police used tear gas to subdue the activists and arrested several.

1971, May 3
1971 May Day Protests

Mass action by Vietnam anti-war militants to shut down the federal government. The 1971 May Day Protests were a series of large-scale civil disobedience actions in Washington, D.C., in protest against the Vietnam War. These began on May Day of that year, continued with similar intensity into the morning of the third day, then rapidly diminished through several following days. Most members of the Nixon Administration would come to view the events as damaging, because the government's response led to mass arrests and were perceived as violating rights.

By the middle of 1970 many leaders of the anti war movement had come to believe that tactics of massive, non-violent political protests that had been used previously would not end the war, and that more aggressive actions were needed. It was decided that small groups of protesters would block major intersections and bridges in the capital.

1972, May 21
Emergency March on Washington

Organized by the National Peace Action Coalition and the People's Coalition for Peace and Justice to protest the U.S.'s increased bombing of North Vietnam and the mining of N.V. harbors. Demonstration draws between 8,000 to 15,000 protesters.

Disillusionment with the war by the U.S. led to the gradual withdrawal of U.S. ground forces as part of a policy known as Vietnamization, which aimed to end American involvement in the war while transferring the task of fighting the Communists to the South Vietnamese themselves. Despite the Paris Peace Accord, which was signed by all parties in January 1973, the fighting continued. As peace protests spread across the United States, disillusionment and ill-discipline grew in the ranks including increased drug use, "fragging" and desertions.

1972, May 27
March to protest apartheid in South Africa

8,000-10,000 attendees. Racial segregation in South Africa began in colonial times under Dutch rule. Apartheid as an officially structured policy was introduced following the general election of 1948. Legislation classified inhabitants into four racial groups, "black", "white", "coloured", and "Indian", with Indian and coloured divided into several sub-classifications, and residential areas were segregated. From 1960 to 1983, 3.5 million non-white South Africans were removed from their homes, and forced into segregated neighbourhoods, in one of the largest mass removals in modern history. Non-white political representation was abolished in 1970, and starting in that year black people were deprived of their citizenship, legally becoming citizens of one of ten tribally based self-governing homelands called bantustans, four of which became nominally independent states.

1973, January 20
Anti-war protest demonstration

Includes the Yippies-Zippie RAT float & SDS, "March Against Racism & the War" contingent.

The Youth International Party, whose members were commonly called Yippies, was a radically youth-oriented and countercultural revolutionary offshoot of the free speech and anti-war movements of the 1960s. It was founded on December 31, 1967. They employed theatrical gestures, such as advancing a pig ("Pigasus the Immortal") as a candidate for President in 1968, to mock the social status quo. They have been described as a highly theatrical, anti-authoritarian and anarchist youth movement of "symbolic politics".

1974, January 22
March for Life

Pro-life demonstration held (annually) on the anniversary of Roe v. Wade. The March for Life is an annual pro-life rally protesting abortion, held in Washington, D.C., on or around the anniversary of the United States Supreme Court's decision legalizing abortion in the case Roe v. Wade. The march is organized by the March for Life Education and Defense Fund. The overall goal of the march is to overturn the Roe v. Wade decision. The 38th annual March for Life occurred on Monday, January 24, 2011-instead of the usual January 22-because Congress is not in session on weekends. The 2013 march was moved to January 25, 2013, to accommodate the Presidential Inauguration. The March for Life typically previously drew around 250,000 attendees each year, with attendance increasing over the past few years.

1974, April 27
Impeachment of President Richard M. Nixon

Ten thousand participants marched for the impeachment of Richard Nixon after the details of the Watergate scandal emerged. Protesters carried signs and marched in front of the White House.

In light of his loss of political support and the near-certainty of impeachment, Nixon resigned the office of the presidency on August 9, 1974, after addressing the nation on television the previous evening. The resignation speech was delivered from the Oval Office and was carried live on radio and television. Nixon stated that he was resigning for the good of the country and asked the nation to support the new president, Gerald Ford. Nixon went on to review the accomplishments of his presidency, especially in foreign policy.

1977, August 26
March for the Equal Rights Amendment

Drew thousands of feminists, including original suffragettes. The Equal Rights Amendment (ERA) was a proposed amendment to the United States Constitution designed to guarantee equal rights for women. The ERA was originally written by Alice Paul and Crystal Eastman. In 1923, it was introduced in the Congress for the first time. In 1972, it passed both houses of Congress and went to the state legislatures for ratification.

The resolution in Congress that proposed the amendment set a ratification deadline of March 22, 1979. Through 1977, the amendment received 35 of the necessary 38 state ratifications. Five states later rescinded their ratifications before the 1979 deadline, though the validity of these rescissions is disputed. In 1978, a joint resolution of Congress extended the ratification deadline to June 30, 1982, but no further states ratified the amendment before the passing of the second deadline.

1978, July 9
March for the Equal Rights Amendment

Drew 100,000 feminist women and men. Upon its introduction, the Equal Rights Amendment stirred up debate about the direction of the ideology and tactics of the women's movement. The National Woman's Party supported the amendment, arguing that women should be on equal terms with men in all regards, even if that means sacrificing certain benefits given to women through protective legislation, such as shorter work hours. However, opponents of the amendment believed that these gender-based benefits protected women as they entered new spheres, such as the work industry, and that the loss of such protection would not be worth the supposed gain in equality. In 1924, The Forum hosted a debate between Doris Stevens and Alice Hamilton concerning these two perspectives on the proposed amendment.

1978, July 11
Longest Walk

Thousands of Native Americans finish their 3200 miles long walk from San Francisco, rallying at the National Mall for religious freedom for traditional American Indians and against eleven drafts discussed at the Congress, and considered anti-Indian by native community.

"The longest walk" (1978) was an AIM-led spiritual walk across the country to support tribal sovereignty and bring attention to 11 pieces of anti-Indian legislation; AIM believed that the proposed legislation would have abrogated Indian Treaties, quantified and limited water rights, etc. The first walk began on February 11, 1978, with a ceremony on Alcatraz Island, where a Sacred Pipe was loaded with tobacco. The Pipe was carried the entire distance.

1979, February 5
Tractorcade

6000 family farmers drove their tractors to Washington D.C. to protest American farm policy. On February 5th, 1979, farmers arrived in Washington, D.C.; 17 tractors had been impounded. Police confined the tractors to the National Mall. They blocked traffic, creating significant tie-ups. A blizzard hit while they were in town, and then the tractors became useful as they were the only vehicles that could reliably travel through the snow, often delivering doctors and nurses to hospitals.

A group of Maryland farmers attempted to repair the damage to the Mall, by sowing grass seed. The Carter administration agreed that the Farmers Home Administration would stop all foreclosures, but soon after the rally was over resumed foreclosures of farms with past due loans.

October 14, 1979
National March on Washington for Lesbian and Gay Rights

First such march on Washington drew 75,000 gay men and lesbians to demand equal civil rights. In addition to the march itself, the organizers arranged three days of workshops featuring artistic events, strategy sessions, focus groups on specific issues of women and minorities within the LGBT community, consciousness raising, local organization, religion and other issues. The Monday after the march was organized as a "Constituent Lobbying Day" in which over 500 participants attempted to contact every member of Congress to express support for gay-rights legislation. The participants successfully met with fifty senators and more than 150 house members.

Organizations supporting the march included Lambda Legal Defense Fund, the National Coalition of Black Lesbians and Gays, the National Gay Task Force (who had withheld their endorsement until only a month prior to the march), the National Organization for Women.

1979, November 9
Iran Hostage Crisis

A sign said "Deport all Iranians" and "Get the hell out of my country". In the United States, the hostage-taking is said to have created "a surge of patriotism" and left "the American people more united than they have been on any issue in two decades". The action was seen "not just as a diplomatic affront", but as a "declaration of war on diplomacy itself". Television news gave daily updates. The respected CBS Evening News anchor, Walter Cronkite, began ending each show in January 1980 by saying how many days the hostages had been captive. President Carter applied economic and diplomatic pressure on Iran: oil imports from Iran were ended on November 12, 1979, and through the issuance of Executive Order 12170, around US$8 billion of Iranian assets in the U.S. were frozen by the Office of Foreign Assets Control on November 14.

1981, March 23
Draft Registration Protest

About 30,000 rally against the renewal of Draft Registration, signed into law by President Jimmy Carter. As the Vietnam War became more unpopular, the draft became more of a focal point for opposition and, despite O'Brien, public protests involving the burning of draft cards proliferated.

In 1980, however, Congress reinstated the requirement that young men register with the Selective Service System, but without reinstating an active draft. In 1984, the Supreme Court upheld the registration requirement against a claim that it violated the privilege against self-incrimination. The following year, it upheld the conviction of a man who refused to register despite his argument that this refusal constituted a political protest.

1981, September 19
Solidarity Day march

AFL-CIO organized march to protest Reagan Administration labor and domestic policies; 260,000 march. Following the firing of the PATCO workers, officials from that union visited various other unions in an attempt to garner support from various other unions. These efforts were not particularly well received because in the 1980 presidential election, PATCO refused to back President Jimmy Carter, instead endorsing Republican Party candidate Ronald Reagan.

The AFL-CIO's Solidarity Day march in Washington, D.C., in September 1981, came a few weeks into the PATCO strike, and drew half a million union people. The solidarity march was even bigger than the great 1968 march. In other ways the march was a new experience in post-war Washington. Because, though many groups and parties supported the demonstration, it was over-whelmingly a demonstration of organised labour. It was the first major demonstration to have been organised for decades by the AFL-CIO.

1982, November 27
Washington Anti-Klan Protest

The John Brown Anti-Klan Committee published a quarterly national newsletter, originally called Death to the Klan, and later renamed No KKK, No Fascist USA!. The paper had a circulation of 10,000 and focused on issues such as the racist nature of tracking in schools, homophobia, and political prisoners. The JBAKC directly confronted white supremacists when they held rallies, and the confrontations sometimes became violent.

As part of their effort to challenge white supremacy, the group worked to clean up anti-Semitic and racist graffiti in the Lincoln Park neighborhood of Chicago. The swastikas and similar graffiti were spray-painted on the 40th anniversary of Kristallnacht, when Jewish-owned businesses across Germany were vandalized. The vandalism was attributed to William G. Leinberger, a member of the neo-Nazi group Chicago Area Skin Heads.

1983, August
March on Washington commemorating the 20th anniversary of the MLK "I Have a Dream" speech

Beginning in 1971, cities such as St. Louis, Missouri, and states established annual holidays to honor King. At the White House Rose Garden on November 2, 1983, President Ronald Reagan signed a bill creating a federal holiday to honor King. Observed for the first time on January 20, 1986, it is called Martin Luther King, Jr. Day. Following President George H. W. Bush's 1992 proclamation, the holiday is observed on the third Monday of January each year, near the time of King's birthday. On January 17, 2000, for the first time, Martin Luther King Jr. Day was officially observed in all fifty U.S. states. Arizona (1992), New Hampshire (1999) and Utah (2000) were the last three states to recognized the holiday. Utah previously celebrated the holiday at the same time but under the name Human Rights Day.

1986, March 1 - November 15
The Great Peace March for Global Nuclear Disarmament

From Los Angeles, California to Washington D.C. (a.k.a. The Great Peace March) to raise awareness of the growing danger of nuclear proliferation and to advocate for complete, verifiable elimination of nuclear weapons from the earth. The March was conceived by Los Angeles businessman David Mixner, who formed People Reaching Out for Peace (PRO-Peace), a non-profit organization. Due to bankruptcy, PRO-Peace folded while the March was in Barstow, California. A few weeks of round-the-clock meetings followed to assess resources, reorganize, and to form a grassroots, self-governed organization. Once reorganized, the March continued its eastward trek.

The GPM consisted of hundreds of people, mostly but not exclusively Americans, who convened in Los Angeles, California, USA, in February 1986 to walk from L.A. to Washington, D.C., the nation's capital. The group left Los Angeles on March 1, 1986 and arrived in Washington, D.C. on November 15, 1986, a journey of about 3,700 miles, nine months, and many campsites.

1987, May 25
Rolling Thunder Run to the Wall

Rolling Thunder is an annual motorcycle demonstration to bring awareness to issues related to American POW/MIA. It has evolved to be a more generic demonstration in support of soldiers and veterans.

Their main annual event occurs on the Sunday before Memorial Day, in which members make a slow ride on a dedicated, closed off, pre-set route, called Ride to the Wall in Washington D.C., referring to the Vietnam Veterans Memorial Wall, also called the Ride for Freedom, which leaves the Pentagon parking lot at noon, crosses the Memorial Bridge, and ends at the Vietnam Veterans Memorial. During the Rolling Thunder weekend, members and supporters spend time at the Thunder Alley (the official vendor site for the event), visit significant areas of Washington D.C., particularly the numerous memorials, and hear speeches given by members, supporters, military officials and politicians.

1987, October 11
Second National March on Washington for Lesbian and Gay Rights

The second such march on Washington drew 500,000 gay men and women to protest for equal civil rights and to demand government action in the fight against AIDS.

The march was part of six days of activities, with a mass wedding and protest in front of the Internal Revenue Service on October 10, and, three days later, a civil disobedience act in front of the Supreme Court building protesting its rulings upholding Bowers v. Hardwick.

The march itself was led by Cesar Chavez and Eleanor Smeal, who were followed by people with AIDS and their supporters. The 200,000 person estimate, widely quoted from the New York Times, was made several hours before the march actually began. Police on the scene estimated numbers during the actual march to be closer to half a million.

1987, December 6
Freedom Sunday Rally on behalf of Soviet Jewry

In December 6, 1987, the American Jewish Committee organized the Freedom Sunday Rally on behalf of Soviet Jewry. 250,000 people attended the D.C. rally, which demanded that the Soviet government allow Jewish emigration from the USSR. [American Jewish Committee]

AJC was active in the campaign to gain emigration rights for Jews living in the Soviet Union and was one of the founders of the American Jewish Conference on Soviet Jewry. In December 1987, AJC's Washington representative, David Harris, who would later become the organization's executive director, organized the Freedom Sunday Rally on behalf of Soviet Jewry. Approximately 250,000 people attended the D.C. rally, which demanded that the Soviet government allow Jewish emigration from the USSR.

1989, April
March for Women's Lives

Sponsored by the National Organization for Women. Attendance estimated at 500,000. The March for Women's Lives was a demonstration for reproductive rights and women's rights, held April 25, 2004 on the National Mall in Washington, D.C.. March organizers estimated that 1.15 million people participated, declaring it "the largest protest in U.S. history"; others estimated no more than 800,000 marchers, with the Associated Press and the BBC putting the figure between 500,000 and 800,000, comparable to the Million Man March of 1995. (The National Park Service no longer makes official estimates of attendance after the Million Man March controversy in 1994, so estimates are unofficial and may be speculative.) Participants protested the recently passed Partial-Birth Abortion Ban Act (2003) as well as other policies they believed to be "anti-women".

1991, January 19 and 26
Dual Marches against the Gulf War

The National Campaign for Peace in the Middle East estimated 250,000 attended the march on the 26th, but the National Park Service estimated attendance at 75,000. The march on January 19 was estimated at 25,000.

Alternative media outlets provided views in opposition to the war. Deep Dish Television compiled segments from independent producers in the U.S. and abroad, and produced a ten-hour series that was distributed internationally, called The Gulf Crisis TV Project. The series' first program War, Oil and Power was compiled and released in 1990, before the war broke out. News World Order was the title of another program in the series; it focused on the media's complicity in promoting the war, as well as Americans' reactions to the media coverage. In San Francisco, as a local example, Paper Tiger Television West produced a weekly cable television show with highlights of mass demonstrations, artists' actions, lectures, and protests against mainstream media coverage at newspaper offices and television stations.

1992, April 5
March for Women's Lives

Pro-choice march organized by the National Organization for Women. The name would be reused for a similar 2004 event. Participants protested the recently passed Partial-Birth Abortion Ban Act (2003) as well as other policies they believed to be "anti-women".

Pro-life counter-protesters, some affiliated with Randall Terry's "Operation Witness", lined a portion of the march route along Pennsylvania Avenue. Terry estimated that there were "over a thousand" counter-protesters; pro-choice writer Jo Freeman estimated that there were "about 300", and the Washington Post wrote that there were "scores". Sixteen protesters from the Christian Defense Coalition were arrested for demonstrating without a permit when they crossed police barricades into the area designated for the March.

1992, May 16
Save our Cities! Save our Children!

Estimates put the crowd at 150,000. Save Our Children was the first organized opposition to the gay rights movement, whose beginnings were traced to the Stonewall riots in 1969. The defeat of the ordinance encouraged groups in other cities to attempt to overturn similar laws. In the next year voters in St. Paul, Minnesota, Wichita, Kansas, and Eugene, Oregon overturned ordinances in those cities, sharing many of the same campaign strategies that were used in Miami. Save Our Children was also involved in Seattle, Washington, where they were unsuccessful, and heavily influenced Proposition 6-a proposed state law in California that would have made the firing of openly gay public school employees mandatory-that was rejected by California voters in 1978.

1993, April 25
March on Washington for Lesbian, Gay and Bi Equal Rights and Liberation

Organizers estimated 1,000,000 attended, but the National Park Service estimated attendance at 300,000. The March on Washington for Lesbian, Gay, and Bi Equal Rights and Liberation was a large political rally that took place in Washington, D.C. on April 25, 1993. Organizers estimated that 1,000,000 attended the March. This was backed up by estimates by the D.C. police, which put the number between 800,000 and more than 1 million attendees.

In the days surrounding the March, a wide range of events serving different subsets of the LGBT community were held throughout Washington, DC. These included historical exhibits, religious services, lobbying events, social gatherings, art exhibits, political workshops, public service events and candlelight vigils.

1995, October 16
Million Man March

The Million Man March was a gathering en masse of African-Americans in Washington, D.C. on October 16, 1995. Called by Louis Farrakhan, it was held on and around the National Mall in the city. The National African American Leadership Summit, a leading group of civil rights activists and the Nation of Islam working in conjunction with scores of civil rights organizations including many local chapters of the National Association for the Advancement of Colored People (but not the national NAACP) formed the Million Man March Organizing Committee. The founder of the National African American Leadership Summit, Dr. Benjamin Chavis, Jr. served as National Director of the Million Man March. United States Park Police officially estimated the crowd size at 400,000 while a Boston University study put the number at 837,000.

1996, October 12
Immigrant Rights March

First national march in D.C. for equal rights for immigrants. In addition to their condemnation of the conditions at immigration detention centers, various human rights groups and news sources have also criticized the high costs necessary to sustain ICE's detention infrastructure. ICE's annual budget is roughly 2.5 billion for its detention and deportation duties. The daily cost for holding an individual at an immigration detention facility is roughly $100 per person. Furthermore, it has been reported that only a small percentage of the population of detained immigrants have committed crimes. Of the 32,000 immigrants in ICE detention on January 25, 2009, 18,690 had no criminal convictions, "not even for illegal entry." Protests by detained immigrants have taken place at several facilities, including the Varick Federal Detention Facility in Manhattan.

1997, October 4
Promise Keepers

Event titled Stand in the Gap: A Sacred Assembly of Men, an open-air gathering at the National Mall. Promise Keepers' most notable event was its Stand in the Gap: A Sacred Assembly of Men open-air gathering at the National Mall in Washington, D.C. on October 4, 1997. C-SPAN carried the event live in its entirety. It was reported at the time to be the largest gathering of men in American history, surpassing even the Million Man March. Attendance at regional rallies where the admission can cost $60 USD has caused some numbers to drop as many men opted to attend the free Washington rallies instead.

Promise Keepers is a Christian organization for men. While it originated in the United States, independent branches are established in Canada and New Zealand.

2000, April 16
Protests of the IMF/World Bank meeting

Supporting march for the A16 street blockades of an IMF/World Bank meeting. The World Bank has long been criticized by non-governmental organizations, such as the indigenous rights group Survival International, and academics, including its former Chief Economist Joseph Stiglitz, Henry Hazlitt and Ludwig Von Mises. Henry Hazlitt argued that the World Bank along with the monetary system it was designed within would promote world inflation and "a world in which international trade is State-dominated" when they were being advocated. Stiglitz argued that the so-called free market reform policies which the Bank advocates are often harmful to economic development if implemented badly, too quickly ("shock therapy"), in the wrong sequence or in weak, uncompetitive economies.

2000, April 30
Millennium March on Washington.

Controversial LBGT political rally. The Millennium March on Washington was an event to raise awareness and visibility of lesbian, gay, bisexual and transgender (LGBT) people and issues of LGBT rights in the US, it was held April 28 through April 30, 2000 in Washington, DC. The Millennium Pride Festival was held prior to the March, it was a huge event that saw thousands flock to the US capital. A march from the Washington Monument to the front lawn of the Capitol took place on April 30, where the crowd was addressed by several members of Congress and, via video, by President Bill Clinton. Estimates of attendance ranged from 200,000 to 1 million people.

2000, May14
Million Mom March

March against gun violence. The Million Mom March was a rally held on Mother's Day, May 14, 2000 in the Washington D.C. National Mall by the Million Mom March organization in order to promote tighter gun control. The march reportedly drew an estimated attendance of 750,000 people at the D.C. location, but with 150,000 to 200,000 people holding satellite events in more than 70 cities across the country, the total number of participants was about a million.

The Million Mom March began as a grassroots movement sparked by Donna Dees-Thomases after she viewed broadcast coverage of the Los Angeles Jewish Community Center shooting in Granada Hills, California. In October 1999 she and several Tri-State activists held a news conference in Manhattan, where they announced their intent to march on Washington. The march was held on May 14, 2000 to coincide with Mother's Day, with the organization reporting a turnout of 750,000 supporters.

2000, August 26
Rev. Al Sharpton organized the "Redeem the Dream" march in Washington DC commemorating the 37th anniversary of Rev. Martin Luther King's "I Have a Dream" speech.

In 1997, King was unanimously elected to head the Southern Christian Leadership Conference (SCLC), a civil rights organization his father founded. King was the fourth president of the group, which sought to fight police brutality and start new local chapters during the first years of his tenure. Under King's leadership, the SCLC held hearings on police brutality, organized a rally for the 37th anniversary of the "I Have a Dream" speech and launched a successful campaign to change the Georgia state flag, which previously featured a large Confederate cross.

Alfred Charles "Al" Sharpton, Jr. is an American Baptist minister, civil rights activist, television/radio talk show host and a trusted White House adviser who, according to 60 Minutes, has "become the president's go-to black leader".

2000, September 2
The Call DC for God's move in this nation

The Call is an organization which sponsors prayer meetings led by Lou Engle along with other Christian leaders pastors in the U.S.. The meetings request prayer and fasting by Christians in protest against issues such as same-sex marriage and legal access to elective abortion. The Call has drawn support from American Evangelical leaders, but has also been criticized for intolerance.

The Call events has been attended by prominent evangelical leaders such as Mike Huckabee, James Dobson, and Tony Perkins. Engle believes that gatherings such as The Call are necessary to prevent Divine judgment from taking place in the United States due to legalized abortion and the acceptance of homosexuality in American culture. 400,000 gathered.

2000, September 26
Brides March Against Domestic Violence

Demonstration of several women in wedding dresses marching to raise domestic violence awareness. The event began after Gladys Ricart was murdered on September 26, 1999. Her ex-boyfriend was the murderer. He shot Ricart a few hours before her wedding to another man. The bride was buried in her wedding gown.

The memorial march is to raise awareness for domestic violence and is an annual event. The march has grown to include men and women who are against familial violence. Domestic violence often occurs because the perpetrator believes that abuse is justified and acceptable, and may produce intergenerational cycles of abuse that condone violence. Awareness, perception, definition and documentation of domestic violence differs widely from country to country. There may be a cycle of abuse during which tensions rise and an act of violence is committed, followed by a period of reconciliation and calm.

2001, January 20
Counter-Inaugural demonstrations against President George W. Bush

Nationally, Bush was both one of the most popular and unpopular presidents in history, having received the highest recorded presidential approval ratings in the wake of the September 11 attacks, as well as one of the lowest approval ratings during the 2008 financial crisis. Internationally, he was a highly controversial figure, with public protests occurring even during visits to close allies, such as the United Kingdom.

The DC Anti-War Network (DAWN) sponsored a mass rally and march at Malcolm X Park (Meridian Hill Park) to protest the inauguration of President George W. Bush. Following a number of speeches, the group marched south on 16th Street NW and east on H Street NW to McPherson Square.

2001, September 29
Anti-Capitalist Convergence

Originally an organized protest to counter planned World Bank and IMF meetings, many protesters backed out after the World Bank and IMF canceled their meetings in the wake of the September 11 attacks. The protest was turned into the first of several protests against the invasion of Afghanistan, the first major action of the post-September 11 anti-war movement.

Generally, Anti-Capitalist Convergences were assembled as umbrella organizations, to coordinate different groups and struggles. However, many have become groups unto themselves. In the wake of the "Battle of Seattle" and a similar resurgence of anti-capitalist protest and organizing, activists in cities such as Seattle; Washington, D.C.; and Chicago formed Convergences to carry out protests more effectively and to ensure that anti-capitalist organizing would continue after major demonstrations had left the city.

2002, October 26
Protests against the Iraq War

Beginning in 2002, and continuing after the 2003 invasion of Iraq, large-scale protests against the Iraq War were held in many cities worldwide, often coordinated to occur simultaneously around the world. After the biggest series of demonstrations, on February 15, 2003, New York Times writer Patrick Tyler claimed that they showed that there were two superpowers on the planet, the United States and worldwide public opinion.

These demonstrations against the war were mainly organized by anti-war organizations, many of whom had been formed in opposition to the invasion of Afghanistan. In some Arab countries demonstrations were organized by the state. Europe saw the biggest mobilization of protesters, including a rally of three million people in Rome, which is listed in the Guinness Book of Records as the largest ever anti-war rally.

2003, January 18
Anti-war Demonstration

On January 18, anti-war demonstrations, focusing particularly but not exclusively on the expected war with Iraq, took place in villages, towns, and cities around the world, including Tokyo, Moscow, Paris, London, Dublin, Montreal, Ottawa, Toronto, Cologne, Bonn, Gothenburg, Florence, Oslo, Rotterdam, Istanbul and Cairo. In New Zealand, thousands rallied in Dunedin and Christchurch, while in Auckland protesters rallied at the Devonport naval base on January 28, opposing the deployment of the frigate HMNZS Te Mana to the Gulf.

NION and ANSWER jointly organized protests in Washington, D.C. and San Francisco. Other protests took place all over the United States, including various smaller places such as Lincoln, Nebraska.

In Washington, "at least tens of thousands", or "several hundred thousand" people demonstrated through the city, ending with a rally at The Mall. Among the speakers was Rev. Jesse Jackson who told the crowd that "We are here because we choose coexistence over coannihilation."

2004, April 25
March for Women's Lives

A pro-choice march; between 500,000 and 1,100,000 attended. The March for Women's Lives was a demonstration for reproductive rights and women's rights, held April 25, 2004 on the National Mall in Washington, D.C.. March organizers estimated that 1.15 million people participated, declaring it "the largest protest in U.S. history"; others estimated no more than 800,000 marchers, with the Associated Press and the BBC putting the figure between 500,000 and 800,000, comparable to the Million Man March of 1995. (The National Park Service no longer makes official estimates of attendance after the Million Man March controversy in 1994, so estimates are unofficial and may be speculative.) Participants protested the recently passed Partial-Birth Abortion Ban Act (2003) as well as other policies they believed to be "anti-women".

2004, October 17
Million Worker March

The Million Worker March was a rally against perceived attacks upon working families in America and what organizers described as millions of jobs lost during the Bush administration with the complicity of the Congress of the United States.

The Million Worker March took place on October 17, 2004 in Washington, DC. An estimated 10,000 demonstrators spent the day on the steps of the Lincoln Memorial listening to speeches and discussing various issues. Organizers presented an array of demands from better wages to an end to the war in Iraq.

Standing where his father gave his "I have a dream" speech, Martin Luther King III told the crowd that civil rights, workers and anti-war activists must come together in common cause.

2005, January 20
Counter-inaugural protests

Demonstrations against George W. Bush's second inauguration. During the rally at Malcolm X Park, members of the Protest Warrior group, several rally participants, and DAWN marshals got into a confrontation. According to Indymedia sources, "Toward the end of the rally, when there were at least 10,000 people in the park, a Protest Warrior led a few 20-something conservative college kids into, (in their own words) 'the belly of the beast' to systematically seek out 'black-block' anarchists among the mass of peaceful demonstrators and flaunt their pro-Bush war signs in order to instigate a conflict."

ANSWER Coalition had secured a permit for a protest along the Parade Route, to be held at 4th Street and Pennsylvania Avenue NW. Due to security procedures in place, signs could only be made of cardboard, posterboard, or cloth, and could be no larger than three feet by 20 feet, and one quarter inch thickness.

2005, September 24
Anti-War in Iraq protest

Protesters from around the country joined the march in Washington, D.C. organized by ANSWER Coalition and United for Peace and Justice to promote peace and an end to the war in Iraq. Organizers claim that around 250,000 people attended the demonstration. Police said that 150,000 was "as good a guess as any". C-SPAN, which broadcast the pre-march speeches, is said to have estimated 500,000. The demonstration route was chosen to be close to the White House, though President George W. Bush was away at the time.

Representative Cynthia McKinney, George Galloway, Carlos Arredondo, Cindy Sheehan, Jesse Jackson, and former U.S. Attorney General Ramsey Clark attended the rally.

The September 24 March also included over 300 members of Military Families Speak Out, which represents about 2,500 military families.

2005, October 15
Millions More Movement

The Millions More Movement was launched by a broad coalition of African American leaders to mark the commemoration of the 10th Anniversary of the Million Man March. A mass march on Washington, DC, was held on October 15, 2005, to galvanize public support for the movement's goals. The march was open to men, women, and children and focused on creating lasting relationships between participating individuals, faith-based organizations, and community institutions.

In An Open Letter on the Millions More Movement, Louis Farrakhan stated in part, "The Millions More Movement is challenging all of us to rise above the things that have kept us divided in the past, by focusing us on the agenda of the Millions More Movement to see how all of us, with all of our varied differences, can come together and direct our energy, not at each other, but at the condition of the reality of the suffering of our people."

2006, March 6
Project MARCH

Project March lobbies for colon cancer screening for all adults through annual marches to build awareness during National Colorectal Cancer Awareness Month. The American Cancer Society's estimates that there will be approximately 50,000 deaths from colorectal cancer in 2009. Discounting skin cancers, colorectal cancer is the third most common cancer found in men and women in the United States. Colorectal cancer is the second-leading cancer killer in the United States with 150,000 Americans expected to be diagnosed this year. It is also one of the only cancer types that is often preventable through screening. Men and women should start to be screened yearly at age 50, and for those with a family history of the disease, screenings should begin earlier.

2007, January 27
Anti-war protest

The January 27, 2007 anti-war protest was an anti-war march sponsored by United for Peace and Justice in Washington, D.C.. The official event consisted of a rally and march at the United States Capitol.

UFPJ had hoped for up to a million people attending, and it was announced at the protest that aerial photography had estimated that at least 500,000 showed up. The Associated Press has stated that the march drew "tens of thousands".

Capitol police stopped the SDS feeder march near the corner of 3rd and Maryland. As the march turned north, police blocked protesters who walked onto the Capitol lawn. Other protesters, both from the march and on the Mall, moved up in support. The Capitol police moved back to the Capitol building. Some participants in this group left graffiti on the Capitol grounds.

2007, March 17
March 17, 2007 anti-war protest

The March 17, 2007 anti-war protest was an anti-war demonstration sponsored by ANSWER Coalition that marched from Constitution Gardens in Washington, D.C. to The Pentagon in Arlington, Virginia. The date was selected to coincide with the fourth anniversary of the invasion of Iraq, and also the 40th anniversary of a similar anti-war march on October 21, 1967. Organizers estimated 15,000 to 30,000 protesters attended, while the police gave informal estimates of 10,000 to 20,000.

Cindy Sheehan, a prominent opponent of the war, and who lost a son in the war, declared, "We want the people in the White House out of our house and arrested for crimes against humanity," and called the president and his military advisers "war criminals."

2007, June 10
June 10, 2007 anti-Israeli occupation protest

The World Says No to Israeli Occupation was held on June 10-11, 2007 to protest Israeli occupation of the Gaza Strip, Palestinian West Bank and East Jerusalem. Nearly 3,000 protesters turned out to protest on the Capitol's west lawn. After the rally, protesters marched to the White House. The goal of the event was to convince the US government to stop aid to Israel and create a policy to end occupation through the UN.

Rally and march against the Israeli occupation of the Palestinian territories for peace and anti-violence. Opposition in the United States to the Israeli occupation is organized by hundreds of organizations, many of them members of the US Campaign to End the Israeli Occupation. These organizations include peace and anti-war, human rights and Arab- and Muslim-Americans groups. Their tactics include education, protest, civil disobedience and lobbying.

2007, September 15
September 15, 2007 anti-war protest

The September 15, 2007 anti-war protest was a march from the White House to the United States Capitol. It was organized by Veterans for Peace and the ANSWER Coalition. Volunteers were recruited for a civil disobedience action, which included a die-in. Volunteers signed up to take on the name of a soldier or civilian who died because of the war, and lay down around the Peace Monument. In attendance were public figures such as Cindy Sheehan and Ralph Nader. Police arrested more than 190 demonstrators who crossed police lines in front of the Capitol. Chemical spray was used by Capitol Police.

The protest march started near the White House in Lafayette Park where many protesters raised placards to show their disapproval of the war and to demand impeachment of the President for war crimes.

2007, October 19 - 20
October Rebellion

October Rebellion was the collective name for the series of protest events surrounding the fall 2007 meetings of the World Bank and International Monetary Fund on October 19 - 20, 2007, in Washington, D.C., United States. The events were organized by the October Coalition. According to the October Coalition's call to action, the group demanded an end to all third world debt using the financial institutions' own resources, the end to structural adjustment policies believed to prioritize profit over the lives of individuals, and an end to social and environmental issues caused by oil and gas production, mining, and certain kinds of infrastructure development.

Early in the day on October 19, an estimated 100 activists demonstrated outside the Washington headquarters of the U.S. Immigration and Customs Enforcement, an agency of the Department of Homeland Security. Demonstrators had assembled to express a critical view of the economic and immigration policies of the United States, while chanting, "No justice, no peace!"

2007, Unnamed date, Unnamed date
Myanmar political protest

March against the strict, Burmese government. Consists of some Americans, Burmese people, and Asian-American Burmese people. During the 2007 street protests, the junta completely shut down internet connectivity from September 29 to October 4. And state-controlled ISPs occasionally applied bandwidth caps to prevent the sharing of video and image files, particularly during politically sensitive events, such as the November 2010 elections.

Prior to September 2011 the government used a wide range of methods to restrict Internet freedom, including legal and regulatory barriers, infrastructural and technical constraints, and coercive measures such as intimidation and lengthy prison sentences. Although the authorities lacked the capacity to pervasively enforce all restrictions, the impact of sporadic implementation and the ensuing chilling effect was profound.

2008, March 19
March 19, 2008 anti-war protest

March 19, 2008 being the fifth anniversary of the United States 2003 invasion of Iraq and in protest and demonstration in opposition to the war in Iraq, anti-war protests were held throughout the world including a series of autonomous actions in the United States' capitol, Washington, D.C. in London, Sydney, Australia and the Scottish city of Glasgow with the later three being organized by the UK-based Stop the War Coalition. Actions included demonstrations at government buildings and landmarks, protests at military installations and student-led street blockades. The protests were notable, in part, for mostly replacing mass marches with civil disobedience - including religious-focused protests - and for utilizing new technologies to both coordinate actions and interface with traditional print and broadcast media.

2008, April 19
National Socialist Movement protest march

On April 19, 2008, the National Socialist Movement marched against illegal immigration. The National Socialist Movement (NSM) is a white nationalist party operating in the United States and around the world. The group was founded in 1974 as the National Socialist American Workers Freedom Movement by Robert Brannen and Cliff Herrington, former members of the American Nazi Party before its decline. The party's chairman is Jeff Schoep, who has held that position since 1994. The group claims to be the largest and most active National Socialist organization in the United States. Although at times classified as a hate group, it refers to itself as a "white civil rights organization." Each state has members in smaller groups within areas known as "regions." The NSM has national meetings and smaller regional meetings.

2008, June 1
Jewish Federation of Greater Washington

The Jewish Federation of Greater Washington hosted a rally at the National Mall on June 1, 2008. Jewish musicians and bands performed to celebrate the 60th birthday celebration of Israel.

Jewish federations can wield a sizable degree of influence in the Jewish communities in which they are located. Many of the local federations hold annual fundraising drives that are expected to raise most of the next year's budgeting for many community programs. In return, in many communities the agencies which receive funding from the federation agree not to engage in major fundraising for themselves for a number of months often called the "primacy period" when the local federation's fundraising has primacy. Decisions made by the local federations can have a great impact on the community, including the opening or closing of programs, staff hirings and firings, and land purchases and sales.

2008, July 11
Longest Walk 2

Hundreds of the Longest Walk 2 participants and supporters from the USA, Canada, Mexico, Japan, Poland, and many Native American nations finish their 8000 miles walk from Alcatraz Island in San Francisco to Washington, D.C. Walkers, gathered to "protect sacred sites", "defend human rights", and "clean Mother Earth" by the American Indian Movement co-founder Dennis Banks and other native leaders, present their Manifesto for a Change to Rep. John Conyers at the Capitol Hill. Two days of pow-wow and concerts at the Mall follow.

The Longest Walk 2 had representatives from more than 100 American Indian nations, and other indigenous participants, such as Maori. It also had non-indigenous supporters. The walk highlighted the need for protection of American Indian sacred sites, tribal sovereignty, environmental protection and action to stop global warming. Participants traveled on either the Northern Route (basically that of 1978) or the Southern Route. Participants crossed a total of 26 states on the two different routes.

2008, July 12
Revolution March

The Revolution March was a rally and march protesting numerous violations of the U.S. Constitution due to the Iraq Invasion, Federal Reserve, Internal Revenue Service, and policies of the Bush Administration. Over 10,000 people marched, participated in the rally, and enjoyed the musical guests. Keynote speaker: Ron Paul, Guest Speakers: Naomi Wolf, G. Edward Griffin, Thomas E. Woods, Jr., Chuck Baldwin and more.

Some observers have noted that the protests against the Iraq war have been relatively small-scale and infrequent compared to protests against the Vietnam War. One of the most often cited factors for this is the lack of conscription. These protests are said to be the biggest global peace protests before a war actually started; the peace movement is compared with the movement caused by the Vietnam War.

2008, July 19
Over 9000 Anonymous March

Project Chanology (also called Operation Chanology) was a protest movement against the practices of the Church of Scientology by members of Anonymous, a leaderless Internet-based group that defines itself as ubiquitous. The project was started in response to the Church of Scientology's attempts to remove material from a highly publicized interview with Scientologist Tom Cruise from the Internet in January 2008.

The project was publicly launched in the form of a video posted to YouTube, "Message to Scientology", on January 21, 2008. The video states that Anonymous views Scientology's actions as Internet censorship, and asserts the group's intent to "expel the church from the Internet".

2008, November 15
Anti-Proposition 8
Protest against the passage of California Proposition 8.

On November 15, 2008, thousands of people in cities across the United States and ten other countries protested California voters' approval of Proposition 8, which changed the state Constitution to restrict the definition of marriage to opposite-sex couples and eliminated same-sex couples' right to marry. The demonstrations were organized by Join the Impact, a grassroots group that emerged in light of the election results.

Proposition 8 was the most expensive proposition in United States history and sharply divided social conservatives and social liberals, as part of the ongoing American culture wars. The ballot initiative was approved by a majority (52%) of voters. Immediately same-sex marriages were halted and the legal status of the 18,000 same-sex couples was thrown into question. Supporters of the proposition included a coalition of religious and social conservatives that felt the court ruling had redefined marriage.

2009, January 10
ANSWER Coalition protest against Israeli bombing of civilians of Gaza.

Act Now to Stop War and End Racism (ANSWER), also known as International A.N.S.W.E.R. and the ANSWER Coalition, is a United States-based protest umbrella group consisting of many antiwar and civil rights organizations. Formed in the wake of the September 11th attacks, ANSWER has since helped to organize many of the largest anti-war demonstrations in the United States, including demonstrations of hundreds of thousands against the Iraq War. The group has also organized activities around a variety of other issues, ranging from the Israel/Palestine debate to immigrant rights to Social Security to the extradition of Luis Posada Carriles.

ANSWER has faced criticism from other anti-war groups for its affiliations, tactics at demonstrations, and allegedly sectarian approach to joint anti-war work. It also faced criticism from various sources for its claimed anti-Zionist politics.

2009, March 19
Funk the War 7

Sponsored by the DC chapter of Students for a Democratic Society, Funk the War 7 was held on the sixth anniversary of the Iraq invasion led by the US. The protest included a protest march and a dance party, as well as visiting the offices of media organizations, think tanks and assorted government offices.

The anti-war march began at Franklin Square and moved through downtown Washington, ending in Dupont Circle. The route passed a number of important organizations and offices, including the Armed Forces Recruitment Center, American Enterprise Institute and the American Petroleum Institute. Code Pink was in attendance, as well as a large number of local activists. Police were also present for the march, to keep protesters on the sidewalk and to block entrances to offices.

2009, March 21
March 21, 2009 anti-war protest

Thousands of protesters marched from the Mall in Washington D.C. to the grounds of the Pentagon, and then to the Crystal City district of Arlington, Virginia. This area of Arlington is the home to offices of several defense contractors, such as KBR and General Dynamics. Protesters carried mock coffins representing the victims of U.S. conflicts and placed them in front of the office buildings. Virginia State police and Arlington County police greeted the protesters and reported no arrests.

Beginning in 2002, and continuing after the 2003 invasion of Iraq, large-scale protests against the Iraq War were held in many cities worldwide, often coordinated to occur simultaneously around the world.

2009, April 15
Tea Party protests

April 15, 2009 is said to have been the day that had the largest number of tea party demonstrations reportedly in more than 750 cities. The Christian Science Monitor reported on the difficulties of calculating a cumulative turnout and said some estimates state that over half a million Americans participated in the protests, noting, "experts say the counting itself often becomes politicized as authorities, organizers, and attendees often come up with dramatically different counts." Grover Norquist, president of Americans for Tax Reform, estimated that at least 268,000 attended in over 200 cities. Statistician Nate Silver, manager of FiveThirtyEight.com, has said that a cumulative crowd size estimate from credible sources was of 311,460 attendees in 346 cities, which accounted for all capitols and major cities little noticeable or no reliable media coverage in other protests could have contributed to a lower number of attendees and locations.

2009, April 25
IMF and World Bank protest march

Over 100 protesters gathered outside the International Monetary Fund (IMG) and World Bank meetings on April 25, 2009. The rally was organized to protest the manner in which world leaders managed the economic crisis. Police were dispatched to remove activists when they attempted to walk down a street that had been placed off limits. Pepper spray and force was used by the protesters.

The IMF is a self-described "organization of 188 countries, working to foster global monetary cooperation, secure financial stability, facilitate international trade, promote high employment and sustainable economic growth, and reduce poverty around the world." The organization's objectives are stated in the Articles of Agreement and can be summarised as: to promote international economic cooperation, international trade, employment, and exchange-rate stability, including by making financial resources available to member countries to meet balance of payments needs.

2009, June 18 - 21
Protest against the disputed Iranian elections

Iran's tenth presidential election was held on 12 June 2009, with incumbent Mahmoud Ahmadinejad running against three challengers. The next morning the Islamic Republic News Agency, Iran's official news agency, announced that with two-thirds of the votes counted, Ahmadinejad had won the election with 62% of the votes cast, and that Mir-Hossein Mousavi had received 34% of the votes cast. There were large irregularities in the results and people were surprised by them, which resulted in protests gathering millions of Iranians in every Iranian city and around the world and the emergence of the opposition Iranian Green Movement.

The Guardian reported on 17 June 2009 that an Iranian news website identified at least 30 polling sites with turnout over 100% and 200 sites with turnout over 95%. On 21 June 2009, a spokesman from the Guardian Council (an organ of the Iranian government) stated that the number of votes cast exceeded the number of eligible voters in no more than 50 cities, something the Council argued was a normal phenomenon which had taken place in previous elections as people are not obliged to vote where registered.

2009, July 4
Tea Party protest

Opposing fiscal policies of Obama administration and Congress. A number of Tea Party protests were held the weekend of July 4, 2009, coinciding with Independence Day. "The rally followed a national effort that drew thousands of activists to Tea Party events across the country on April 15, 2009 when income taxes are due."

Most Tea Party activities have since been focused on opposing efforts of the Obama Administration, and on recruiting, nominating, and supporting candidates for state and national elections. The name "Tea Party" is a reference to the Boston Tea Party, whose principal aim was to protest taxation without representation. Tea Party protests evoked images, slogans and themes from the American Revolution, such as tri-corner hats and yellow Gadsden "Don't Tread on Me" flags.

2009, September 12
Taxpayer March on Washington

The Tea Party protests were a series of protests throughout the United States that began in early 2009. The protests were part of the larger political Tea Party movement.

On September 12, 2009, Tea Party protests were held in various cities around the nation. In Washington, D.C., Tea Party protests gathered to march from Freedom Plaza to the United States Capitol. Estimates of the number of attendees varied, from "tens of thousands" to "in excess of 75,000". A rally organizer asserted that one local ABC News station had reported attendance of over one million, but he retracted the statement after ABC News denied making any such report.

Using the counts of those in attendance, the march may have been the largest conservative protest ever held in Washington, D.C., as well as the largest demonstration against President Obama's administration to date.

2009, October 11
National Equality March

Approximately 200,000 people demonstrated in support of equal protection for lesbian, gay, bisexual, and transgender people. The National Equality March was a national political rally that occurred October 11, 2009 in Washington, D.C. It called for equal protection for lesbian, gay, bisexual, and transgender (LGBT) people in all matters governed by civil law in all 50 states and the District of Columbia. The march was called for by activist David Mixner and implemented by Cleve Jones, and organized by Equality Across America and the Courage Campaign. Kip Williams and Robin McGehee served as co-directors. Leaders like actress Michelle Clunie and New York gubernatorial aide Peter Yacobellis hosted the first fundraiser in the spring of 2010. This was the first national march in Washington, D.C. for LGBT rights since the 2000 Millennium March.

2010, March 20
March 20, 2010 anti-war protest

On March 20, 2010, a multi-city anti-war event was held in the United States to protest the U.S. wars in Afghanistan and Iraq. The event was organized by A.N.S.W.E.R. with support from other civil society actors such as the Topanga Peace Alliance and the Teamsters. The scheduling of the event ties it to the seventh anniversary of the start of the U.S. invasion of Iraq in 2003. In Washington, D.C. thousands marched past the White House, some bearing coffins draped with various flags to symbolize fatalities of the wars. Others enacted mock attacks on the White House using cardboard combat drones.

ANSWER characterizes itself as anti-imperialist, and its steering committee consists of socialists, civil rights advocates, and left-wing or progressive organizations from the Muslim, Arab, Palestinian, Filipino, Haitian, and Latin American communities.

2010, March 21
March for America

The March for America was a protest march in Washington, DC, United States. On March 21, 2010, over 200,000 marched by the Capitol in Washington, DC, to call for comprehensive immigration reform in that year. The event was organized by Reform Immigration FOR America and many more groups.

Participants largely wore white and waved the United States flag.

President Barack Obama delivered a video message to the assembled crowd, pledging to be their partner in seeking comprehensive immigration reform and fix the country's broken immigration system.

Immigration reform is a term used in political discussion regarding changes to current immigration policy of a country. In the political sense, "immigration reform" may include promoted, expanded, or open immigration, as well as reduced or eliminated immigration.

2010, August 28
Restoring Honor Rally

Cosponsored by Special Operations Warrior Foundation and promoted as a "celebration of America's heroes and heritage." The
number of attendees is disputed. Event organizer Glenn Beck also
held an event at the Kennedy Center called "Divine Destiny"
focused more on faith and religion on 8/27.

Beck's speech at the rally emphasized the theme that Americans
of all religions should turn to their faith in God, "turning our face
back to the values and principles that made us great." Beck's and
Palin's speeches praised George Washington, Abraham Lincoln,
and Martin Luther King Jr., as well as American war veterans. Beck
called for Americans to unite despite political or religious disagree-
ments, with 240 clergy from different races and religions - belong-
ing to the ecumenical ministerial group, the Black Robe Regiment -
joining the events' speakers on stage before its closing statements.

2010, September 27
Appalachia Rising

For years, Julia Bonds dreamed of a "thousand hillbilly march" in Washington, DC. In September 2010, that dream became a reality as thousands marched on the White House for "Appalachia Rising'", a mass movement to persuade US Congress to halt to the issuance of valley fill and other types of permits that allow companies to completely remove a mountain top in the search for coal.

A march of 4,000 residents from across Appalachia, to the EPA and the White House, demanding an end to destructive Mountaintop Removal mining practices. About 113 people were arrested in front of the White House as part of a direct action protest, including Jim Hansen, known as the father of the global warming movement.

\

2010, October 2
One Nation Working Together March for Jobs, Peace and Justice

The One Nation Working Together rally was held on October 2, 2010 in Washington, D.C. by a coalition of liberal and progressive organizations operating under the umbrella of "One Nation Working Together". It was held on the steps of the Lincoln Memorial to demand better jobs, immigration and education reform and as an "antidote" to the Tea Party movement.

With crowds assembling as early as 6:00 AM EST, the rally began with an interfaith service at 11:00 AM, followed by the beginning of musical performances by various recording artists and groups at noon. The event progressed with a series of speeches by various figures before concluding at 4:00 PM.

The rally attracted criticism from the right because the Communist Party USA and International Socialist Organization were among the 400 sponsors who endorsed the rally.

2010, October 30
Rally to Restore Sanity and/or Fear

Held by talk show hosts Jon Stewart and Stephen Colbert to oppose radical political trends in American politics. A crowd estimate commissioned by CBS News by AirPhotosLive.com estimated 215,000 people attended, with a margin of error of plus or minus 10 percent. According to Brian Stelter of the New York Times, the National Park Service privately told Viacom there were "well over 200,000" people present.

The rally was a combination of what initially were announced as separate events: Stewart's "Rally to Restore Sanity" and Colbert's counterpart, the "March to Keep Fear Alive." Its stated purpose was to provide a venue for attendees to be heard above what Stewart described as the more vocal and extreme 15-20% of Americans who "control the conversation" of American politics, the argument being that these extremes demonize each other and engage in counterproductive actions, with a return to sanity intended to promote reasoned discussion.

2010, December 16
Veterans for Peace rally in Lafayette Park and on the White House sidewalk

131 people arrested for blocking the view of the White House per 36 CFR 7.96 (g)(5)(viii), the "ten yards" rule, upheld in 1984-5271 in the White House Vigil for the ERA v. Clark, as a time-place-manner exception to the First Amendment, to achieve a fundamental purpose of the Park Service specified in USC16 article 1.

Veterans For Peace is a United States organization founded in 1985. Made up of US military veterans of World War II, the Korean War, the Vietnam War, the Gulf War, and other conflicts, as well as peacetime veterans and non-veterans, the group works to promote alternatives to war. The organization has opposed the military policies of the United States, NATO and Israel, and has opposed military actions and threats to Russia, Iraq, Afghanistan, Iran, Libya and Syria.

2011, October 16
The Right2Know March for Genetically Engineered Foods (GMO) to be labeled in the United States

In the mid-2000s, a parliamentary review process to replace apartheid laws included a planned repeal and replacement of the Protection of Information Act 84 of 1982.

Critics of the new bill, most notably led by a civil society coalition called the Right2Know Campaign, have broadly accepted the need to replace the 1982 Act, human rights activists, legal experts, opposition parties and a wide range of civil society bodies argued that the Bill does not correctly balance these competing principles, and point to a number of provisions that undermine the right to access information and the rights of whistleblowers and journalists.

The march left New York City on October 1 and arrived after marching 313 miles to the White House. More than 1000 people participated in the march.

2011, October 15
Jobs and Justice March to protest poverty, homelessness and high unemployment

Several thousand protesters marched to protest unemployment, poverty and homelessness. The rally was organized by the National Action Network and the cooperation of several labor and civil rights groups. Prior to the march, the protesters met on the lawn in front of the Washington Monument and held up protest signs.

The rally was meant to encourage the Senate to pass the American Jobs Act, which had been blocked a week before the protest. Rev. Sharpton gave a speech, letting Congress know that the people would rise up against them if they didn't pass the act. The march then moved to the Freedom Monument, where the protests continued.

2011, November 9-23
Occupy Wall Street

Protesters march from New York City to Washington DC, to demonstrate at a congressional committee meeting to decide whether to keep President Barack Obama's extension of tax cuts enacted under former President George W. Bush. Protesters say the cuts benefit only rich Americans.

The main issues raised by Occupy Wall Street were social and economic inequality, greed, corruption and the perceived undue influence of corporations on government-particularly from the financial services sector. The OWS slogan, "We are the 99%", refers to income inequality and wealth distribution in the U.S. between the wealthiest 1% and the rest of the population. To achieve their goals, protesters acted on consensus-based decisions made in general assemblies which emphasized direct action over petitioning authorities for redress.

2012, January 11
Close Guantanamo

271 people in jumpsuits marched from the White House to the Supreme Court, along with 750 others not in jumpsuits.

The Guantanamo Bay detention camp, also referred to as Guantánamo or GTMO, pronounced gitmo, is a United States military prison located within Guantanamo Bay Naval Base, which fronts on Guantánamo Bay in Cuba. At the time of its establishment in January 2002, Secretary of Defense Donald H. Rumsfeld said the prison camp was established to detain extraordinarily dangerous prisoners, to interrogate prisoners in an optimal setting, and to prosecute prisoners for war crimes. Detainees captured in the War on Terror, most of them from Afghanistan and much smaller numbers later from Iraq, the Horn of Africa and Southeast Asia were transported to the prison.

2012, February 20
Veterans Support Ron Paul, March on the White House

Approximately 320 - 558 Veterans and active duty Veterans
Marched, with a double duce truck vehicle carrying Disabled
Veterans including, one of the last WW2, battle of the bulge
Veterans, with another 1500 not formally in the march supporting
behind the march. Upon arriving at the White House, the veterans
and active military service members turned their backs to symboli-
cally signify that they didn't condone all these unconstitutional
wars. There was an eight-minute hand salute for every active duty
military member who had committed suicide under Obama (one
second for each life taken: approximately 480). These numbers are
higher than they have ever been, especially when you include veterans. There were also 21 minutes of silence observed for those
fallen in battle (one second for each life lost: approximately 1,260).
There was a rally for 2 hours before the march at the Washington
Memorial and a 6 hour after party at the rock n roll hotel.

2012, November 3
Million Puppet March

Approximately 1,500 people and puppets marched in support of continued funding for public broadcasting. The march was later recognized as the largest puppet march by Record Setter.

Co-organized by Michael Bellavia and Chris Mecham, the march was inspired by the comments of Presidential hopeful Mitt Romney who promised to end funding for public broadcasting. Bellavia and Mecham viewed Romney's threat as a straw man argument on the issue of the Federal budget and a dog whistle to ultra-conservatives meant to convey his position on social issues.

The march, which drew some 1500 participants, received recognition from Record Setter as the largest puppet march. Participants included Bread and Puppet Theater, Beale Street Puppets, the cast of STUFT, and Craig Aaron, Executive Director of Free Press.

2012, November 17
Move:DC

Approximately 10,000 people marched around the White House to call for an end to the LRA in Central Africa, with the march concluding at the Washington Monument. The march and rally were organized by Invisible Children as a part of the Kony 2012 campaign.

Invisible Children, Inc. is an organization founded in 2004 to bring awareness to the activities of the Lord's Resistance Army (LRA) in Central Africa, and its leader, Joseph Kony. Specifically, the group seeks to put an end to the practices of the LRA which include abductions and abuse of children, and forcing them to serve as soldiers. To this end, Invisible Children urges the United States government to take military action in the central region of Africa.

2013, February 17
Forward on Climate

An estimated 40,000 people rallied on the Mall and marched to the White House demanding action on Climate Change from President Barack Obama and the US Government.

The Forward on Climate rally was held at the National Mall in Washington, D.C. on February 17, 2013. The goal of the demonstration was to spur President Barack Obama and Congress to take more action to address climate change. Opposition to the proposed expansion of the Keystone XL Pipeline, that was still pending at the time, was a particular focus of the rally. Among the speakers were Sierra Club Director Michael Brune, U.S. Senator Sheldon Whitehouse, actress and activist Rosario Dawson, 350.org founder Bill McKibben, and Obama's former Special Advisor for Green Jobs Van Jones.

2013, September 7
NO War Against Syria

Over 500 people gathered to demand an end to the drive to war. Organized by the ANSWER Coalition, the protest was supported by a wide range of organizations including Code Pink, United National Anti-war Coalition and the All-African People's Revolutionary Party.

About ten activists of Code Pink demonstrated in U.S. Congress against military attacks in retaliation for Syria's suspected use of chemical weapons against its own people. Code Pink: Women for Peace is a NGO that describes itself as a "grassroots peace and social justice movement working to end U.S.-funded wars and occupations, to challenge militarism globally, and to redirect our resources into health care, education, green jobs and other life-affirming activities". It is primarily focused on anti-war issues, but has also taken positions on gun control, social justice, Palestinian statehood, green jobs and health care issues.

2013, October 13
"Million Vet March"

Thousands of protesters expressed their dissatisfaction over the closure of national memorials honoring the service of American veterans in combat administered by the National Park Service which have been officially closed due to the United States federal government shutdown of 2013. Protesters removed barricades (or "Barrycades" as coined by the protesters) from the National World War II Memorial and brought them to the fence surrounding the White House. Senator Ted Cruz and Sarah Palin made appearances at this rally.

The protesters sang "God Bless America" and chanted "tear down these walls" as they removed the barricades. Ted Cruz asked why the government was spending money to prevent veterans from entering the memorial.

Unprecedented Access To
Government Representatives

Send a Message to 100 Different
State & Federal Politicians Each day

Burroughs Media developed **ThePeopleGov.org**, a free site, that gives a voice back to the average citizen who can now reach 100's of state and/or federal government representative in a few clicks. Reach 5000 representatives in 10 seconds if 10 people send 100 messages each day for 5 days.

There are other sites on the Internet to contact government officials, but you have to do it one at a time and often the contact information is buried 2-3 levels down.

People have busy lives, making a living. They need an easy and powerful way to be heard by their state and federal legislatures and hopefully get a message across about changing or creating laws and other concerns. With ThePeopleGov.org we hope to revitalize our democracy.

President of Burroughs Media, Trace Burroughs states, "This new, easy

to navigate free site will give the power back to the people - the foundation on which the United States was created; a gove rmment run by the people and not by special interest or corporate money. We have strayed from true democracy, but we can get it back.

We set an example for the rest of the world and they are watching us. We have no agenda with ThePeopleGov.org and it's open to all people no matter what their cause is or law they want passed in Washington or their state. We believe if U.S. citizens regain their power to be heard in an easy and powerful way, good things will happen.

This is a service free to the community. If enough people participate, it's like a cyber march on Washington.

Online Resource: Petitioning the Government

We the People: Your Voice in Our Government
https://petitions.whitehouse.gov/

Has over 23 million members.
http://www.thepetitionsite.com/

How to write a local government petition.
http://www.wikihow.com/Write-a-Petition

World's largest online campaigning platform.
https://www.causes.com/

78,163,323 people taking action
https://www.change.org/

The top site for conservative causes.
http://www.ipetitions.com/red-petitions

Liberal/progresive issues. 8 million MoveOn members.
http://petitions.moveon.org/

Sources

Quotes About Nonviolence
http://www.brainyquote.com/quotes/keywords/non-violence.html

History of Nonviolent Protests and The Basic Elements
of Nonviolence
http://www.actupny.org

198 Methods of Nonviolent Action
http://www.aforcemorepowerful.org/resources/nonviolent/
methods.php

Organizing Small and Large Protests
http://www.occupytogether.org/blog/2012/06/15/how-to-organize-
a-protest

Organizing a March on Washington
http://www.ehow.com/how_2051467_organize-protest-
washington-dc.html

Historic Non Violent Protests & Marches on Washington
Wikipedia.com

www.ingramcontent.com/pod-product-compliance
Lightning Source LLC
Chambersburg PA
CBHW060612290526
45793CB00001B/4